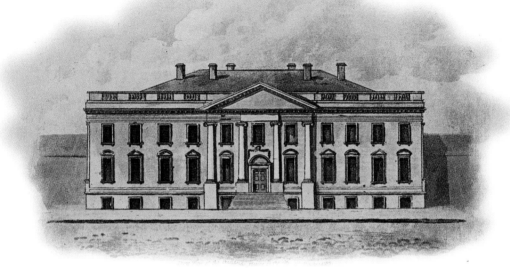

The Entrance Hall seen from the North Portico, with emblems of office at the door of the Blue Room:

THE WHITE HOUSE
AN HISTORIC GUIDE

WHITE HOUSE
HISTORICAL
ASSOCIATION
*with the
cooperation
of the
National
Geographic
Society
Washington, D. C.*

the Presidential seal, the Presidential flag, and the flag of the United States.

WHITE HOUSE HISTORICAL ASSOCIATION
A nonprofit organization, chartered on November 3, 1961, to enhance understanding, appreciation, and enjoyment of the Executive Mansion. Income from the sale of this book will be used to publish other materials about the White House, as well as for the acquisition of historical furnishings and other objects for the Executive Mansion. Address inquiries to 740 Jackson Place, N.W., Washington, D. C. 20503.

THE WHITE HOUSE: AN HISTORIC GUIDE
Produced by the National Geographic Society as a public service
Gilbert M. Grosvenor, *President and Chairman of the Board*
Reg Murphy, *Executive Vice President*
Michela A. English, *Senior Vice President*
PREPARED BY THE BOOK DIVISION
William R. Gray, *Vice President and Director*
Charles Kogod, *Assistant Director*
STAFF FOR THE FIRST EDITION
Robert L. Breeden, *Editorial Director*
Jody Bolt, *Art Director*
Geraldine Linder, *Illustrations Research*
Margaret B. Klapthor, Curator Emeritus, Division of Political History, National Museum of American History, Smithsonian Institution; and Dr. Richard L. Watson, Jr., Professor Emeritus of History, Duke University, *Text Consultants*
Steve Adams, Joseph H. Bailey, James P. Blair, Victor R. Boswell, Jr., David R. Bridge, Nelson Brown, John E. Fletcher, Larry Kinney, Joseph D. Lavenburg, Philip R. Leonhardi, Bates W. Littlehales, George F. Mobley, Robert S. Oakes, Winfield I. Parks, Jr., Tom M. Pope, *Photography*
REVISION STAFF
Jane H. Buxton, *Project Editor;* Elizabeth W. Fisher, *Text Editor;* Robin Tunnicliff, *Researcher;* Suez Kehl, *Art Director;* Lisa Biganzoli, *Artist;* Bryan K. Knedler, *Indexer;* Jack E. Boucher (HABS), Erik Kvalsvik, *Photography;* Elizabeth G. Jevons, Sandra F. Lotterman, Peggy J. Oxford, *Staff Assistants*
MANUFACTURING AND QUALITY MANAGEMENT
George V. White, *Director;* Clifton M. Brown III, *Assistant Manager/Film Archivist*

White House staff members who assisted in preparing this edition: Rex Scouten, *Curator;* Betty C. Monkman, *Associate Curator;* William G. Allman, *Assistant Curator;* Lydia S. Tederick, *Curatorial Assistant*

All objects of art and furniture pictured in this book belong to the White House collection, unless otherwise noted.

Copyright © 1962, 1963, 1964, 1966, 1968, 1969, 1971, 1973, 1975, 1977, 1979, 1982, 1987, 1991, 1994, 1995 White House Historical Association
Nineteenth Edition, 1995
Library of Congress Catalog Card Number 95-61703;
   ISBN 0-912308-60-5 (paperback), 0-912308-61-3 (hardback)

"The Avenue in the Rain," painted in 1917, is one of Childe Hassam's many studies of flags displayed along New York City's Fifth Avenue. It now hangs in the President's Oval Office.
FRONT COVER: *Bright tulips encircle the fountain on the North Lawn in springtime.*
BACK COVER: *At twilight, illuminated fountains splash before the South Portico.*
FRONTISPIECE: *"Front View of the President's House in the City of Washington": This 1807 print is the earliest known of the mansion.*

FOREWORD

America's White House bears the stamp of every President. George Washington chose the site and approved the architectural design. The building was still incomplete when the first residents, John and Abigail Adams, moved in. Soon they, too, put their mark on it, as would each succeeding First Family.

This official guide is in its 19th edition. The first one, which appeared in 1962, was planned by Mrs. John F. Kennedy to help visitors, as she put it, "sort out the impressions received on an often crowded visit." Intensely interested in the book, she personally reviewed all illustrations and text as it took shape. At that time, Congress had voted legislation to preserve the priceless possessions of the White House. Additionally, the nonprofit White House Historical Association had been formed to enhance understanding and appreciation of the Executive Mansion.

An early task of the Historical Association was to publish the guidebook, with the cooperation of the National Geographic Society, which provided photographic and editorial staffs as a public service. All net proceeds from its sale are used to acquire furnishings and art, often linked with past Presidents and the White House, and to support related publications and restoration programs. Private donations of Federal-period furniture and American paintings have aided these efforts.

I am proud to have worked on the White House guidebook since its beginnings—first on its editorial staff and then as an officer of the National Geographic Society and of the White House Historical Association. This sentiment was shared by my colleague the late Melville Bell Grosvenor, who, as Editor of *National Geographic*, was responsible for the participation of the Society in preparing the guide. The Society's current President, Gilbert M. Grosvenor, continues the tradition. Donald J. Crump, former Director of the Geographic's Special Publications Division and now the Association's Director of Publications, has worked on every edition and is due credit for its consistent excellence.

October 13, 1992, marked the 200th anniversary of the laying of the White House cornerstone. The Presidential proclamation celebrating that historic event was first read to scholars from across the nation at an Association-sponsored symposium on the mansion's history. It reminded them: "Much of our Nation's history has passed through these walls, and it is here that much of our future will be shaped as well."

President and Mrs. Clinton take pleasure in welcoming each and every visitor to the White House. We hope that those who visit will rediscover American history at this national center of political, social, and family life.

Robert L. Breeden

Robert L. Breeden
Chairman and Chief Executive Officer
White House Historical Association

The President and I welcome you to the White House.

Each time we walk through these magnificent rooms, we are reminded of the history of our great nation. Each work of art, each highly polished antique, every carefully restored architectural detail speaks to us of the families who have preceded us in this residence.

From the family of John Adams, the first to occupy the White House, to our family today, each presidential family has brought to the house interests and a style uniquely its own. The challenge—and the obligation—is to provide a comfortable family residence and yet maintain the historic presence and integrity of this structure that is so appropriately called *the house of the people*.

The White House is our family's home. For us, as they have for generations of presidential families, its gracious rooms and beautiful gardens welcome family and friends, as well as the million and a half visitors who come each year to see this very special symbol of our country and government. It gives us great pleasure to invite you to visit the house, to enjoy the ambiance of its rooms, and to experience for yourself this national treasure.

Hillary Rodham Clinton

Hillary Rodham Clinton

CONTENTS

A GUIDE TO THE MANSION

BY WENDY CORTESI

More than a million visitors go through the White House every year, making it the most frequently toured home in this country. The only residence of a head of state open to the public on a regular basis free of charge, the White House is a museum of American history—with portraits of Presidents and First Ladies, works by some of America's finest artists, antique furniture in period settings, and memorabilia of historic importance. It is also the home and office of the President of the United States, where the pressing business of government is being conducted even as tourists visit nearby, admiring the mansion's many treasures from the past.

A painting on pages 102-3 of this book indicates the route of the tour through the White House and the locations of the most important rooms. Each tour begins in the wood-paneled East Wing Lobby and continues along the Ground Floor Corridor, up the wide marble staircase, and through the elegant rooms of the State Floor. Portraits of recent Presidents hang in the Cross and Entrance Halls, as well as along the Grand Staircase.

The first part of this book, "A Guide to the Mansion," describes, with historical notes, rooms open to the public and many that are not—some of the private family rooms on the second floor and the Presidential offices in the West Wing. The second part, "The Changing White House," traces, in illustrations and in words, the history of the mansion from its inception on the drawing board of architect James Hoban in 1792 through its many renovations.

Curving walk and driveway—shaded in spring by flowering magnolias— lead to the covered entranceway of the East Wing of the White House. Public tours of the Executive Mansion begin in the East Wing Lobby.

9

THE
EAST
COLONNADE

The Jacqueline Kennedy Garden on the east side of the White House serves primarily as an informal reception area for the First Lady. Flowering trees, shrubs, herbs, and colorful plantings that change with the seasons surround a rectangular lawn. A holly osmanthus hedge and a row of lindens provide shade for the colonnade that connects the East Wing with the mansion.

Most visitors to the White House enter through the East Wing Lobby, then walk through the East Garden Room to the glass-enclosed colonnade that leads to the Ground Floor of the White House. Construction of the East Wing began under Theodore Roosevelt. New York architect Charles McKim, hired to renovate the mansion, designed the East Wing as an entrance for social functions. Completed in 1903, the building changed little until the Franklin D. Roosevelt Administration, when it was enlarged to provide office space.

Portraits of Presidents hang in the lobby. The oil of President Zachary Taylor by Joseph Henry Bush was given to the White House by the President's daughter Betty Taylor Dandridge. Beyond the lobby and up a few steps is the East Garden Room.

To the right is the entrance to the colonnade, constructed in 1902 on the foundations of the original pavilion built by Thomas Jefferson and removed in 1866. Along the colonnade visitors have a view of the Jacqueline Kennedy Garden, so named by Mrs. Lyndon B. Johnson in 1965. A massive bronze bust of Abraham Lincoln by Gutzon Borglum, the sculptor of Mount Rushmore, rests in a wall niche at the east end of the colonnade.

Julia Gardiner Tyler suggested to
President Andrew Johnson that
he begin a collection of portraits
of Presidents' wives—the term
"First Lady" had not yet come into
use—for display in the Executive
Mansion. Johnson agreed and asked
Mrs. Tyler to start the tradition.
On the back of the portrait she
donated, begun in 1846, artist
Francesco Anelli inscribed:
"Mrs. Giulia Gardiner Tyler, in
her 26 year," using the Italian
spelling of her first name.

A Sheraton-style breakfront bookcase, made in Baltimore in the period 1800-10, displays a selection of Presidential china and glass. During the administration of Theodore Roosevelt, the Ground Floor Corridor had several cabinets that held the White House china collection, started by Caroline Scott Harrison in 1889 and greatly expanded by Mrs. Roosevelt. It had grown so large by 1917 that Edith Bolling Galt Wilson placed it in a special area known today as the China Room. On the left of the top shelf is a plate used by George Washington when he was President; the third shelf down contains Lincoln china.

GROUND FLOOR CORRIDOR

Until 1902 the Ground Floor Corridor and the rooms opening off it were used as a work area. When Abraham Lincoln arrived at the White House in 1861, an aide recalled, the basement had "the air of an old and unsuccessful hotel." Even in the cold weather it reminded you "of old country taverns, if not of something you have smelled in the edge of some swamp."

Checking structural conditions in 1902, the New York architectural firm of McKim, Mead & White found that James Hoban's "fine, groined arches . . . had been cut into in all directions" to hold pipes. The furnace room jutted into the corridor; heat mains and a fresh-air duct hung from the ceiling. As a result of the 1902 renovation and extensive re-modeling during the Truman Administration, Hoban's elegant vaulted ceiling was restored to its clean simplicity and the hall transformed by walls and floors of marble. Three bronze-and-crystal Regency chandeliers now light the gallery.

Flanking the stairway to the State Floor are busts of George Washington and Benjamin Franklin, based on works by Houdon. They, and the likenesses of Abraham Lincoln and Thomas Jefferson on the opposite wall, were gifts of the French Republic. Bronze figures of Henry Clay and Daniel Webster by Thomas Ball are displayed on either side of the doorway to the Diplomatic Reception Room. Directly across the hall are two bronze heads: British Prime Minister Winston Churchill by Jacob Epstein and President Dwight D. Eisenhower by Nison Tregor. Two sculptures with Western themes, by Frederic Remington and Charles Russell, stand beside the entrance from the East Foyer.

The Baltimore breakfront bookcase in the corridor contains pieces of White House china and glass. Toward the west end of the hall is the only surviving example of the four pier tables purchased for the East Room in 1829. It bears the label of its maker, Anthony G. Quervelle.

The custom of hanging portraits of First Ladies in this area dates from 1902, when Mrs. Theodore Roosevelt wrote to Charles McKim asking that "all the ladies of the White House, including myself," be relegated to "the downstairs corridor. . . ." Traditionally, portraits of recent First Ladies have been displayed on either side of the entrance to the Diplomatic Reception Room. On the right is Felix de Cossio's portrait of Elizabeth Bloomer Ford and on the left is Rosalynn Smith Carter, painted by George Augusta. Aaron Shikler's portrait of Nancy Davis Reagan hangs at the east end of the corridor. At the west end are portraits of Edith Bolling Galt Wilson by Adolfo Muller-Ury and Mamie Dowd Eisenhower by Thomas E. Stephens, as well as Anders Zorn's 1899 portrait of Frances Folsom Cleveland, on loan from the National Portrait Gallery.

The Ground Floor Corridor provides an elegant gallery for visitors to the White House. James Hoban's original design included groined arches on a vaulted ceiling. The porcelain busts of George Washington and Benjamin Franklin flanking the stairway leading to the State Floor, and Thomas Jefferson across the hall, were gifts of the French Republic.

*While visiting Washington in 1984,
Rosalynn Smith Carter posed for George
Augusta in historic Blair House. Mrs.
Carter used her influence as First Lady
in behalf of women's rights and
programs for the mentally ill. She
spoke of herself as "more a political
partner than a political wife," and she
served as the President's personal
emissary to Latin America and stood in
for him on ceremonial occasions.*

*In his 1987 portrait, Aaron Shikler portrayed Nancy
Davis Reagan in the Red Room. As First Lady,
Mrs. Reagan supported the Foster Grandparent Program,
the subject of her book* To Love A Child. *She focused
attention on drug abuse among young people, and
First Ladies from 17 countries attended her 1985
conference to seek solutions to the global problem. In her
1989 book,* My Turn, *Mrs. Reagan described the joys
and sorrows of her life in the White House.*

In his portrait of Elizabeth Bloomer Ford, painted in 1977 at the Fords' home in Vail, Colorado, Felix de Cossio captures her poise and forthrightness as First Lady. Not hesitating to state her views publicly, she strongly supported the Equal Rights Amendment.

Patricia Ryan Nixon sat for Henriette Wyeth Hurd in San Clemente, California, in 1978. As First Lady, she initiated spring and fall garden tours and candelight Christmas tours of the White House for the public.

"Coming Through the Rye," a bronze sculpture by Frederic Remington that was cast in 1918, depicts four spirited cowboys reveling at full gallop. An Easterner, Remington lived and traveled in the West and left a vivid record of its rugged life in his paintings and sculpture.

THE LIBRARY

The Library was completely redecorated in 1962 as a "painted" room typical of the early 1800's and was refurbished again in 1976. The paneling, now a soft gray color, dates from the Truman renovation of 1948-52. Old timber removed when the mansion was stripped to a shell was made into paneling for various Ground Floor rooms. Over the mantel hangs a Gilbert Stuart portrait of George Washington, painted about 1805, which was donated to the White House in 1949. Right: portraits by Charles Bird King of Indian emissaries who visited the mansion in 1822 — Hayne Hudjihini, or "Eagle of Delight," of the Oto Tribe, who contracted measles during her visit and died shortly after she returned home, and Sharitarish, or "Wicked Chief," of the Pawnee Tribe.

"Tubs, Buckets and a variety of Lumber" cluttered Room 17 of the basement in February 1801, according to the first official White House inventory. The room served mainly as a laundry area until Theodore Roosevelt's renovation of the Ground Floor in 1902, when it was designated a "Gentlemen's Ante-room." In 1935, it was remodeled as a library, and in 1961 a committee was appointed to select works representative of a full spectrum of American thought and tradition for the use of the President, his family, and his staff. This wide-ranging collection is still being augmented with Presidential papers.

The Library is furnished in the style of the late Federal period (1800-1820) with most of the pieces attributed to the New York cabinetmaker Duncan Phyfe. It is less formal than the rooms of the State Floor and is often used for small teas and meetings. The soft gray and rose tones of the paneling are complemented by a Tabriz carpet of the mid-19th century. The gilded wood chandelier with a painted red band was made about 1800 and belonged to the family of James Fenimore Cooper, author of *The Last of the Mohicans* and other classics.

An unusual Federal-period looking glass hangs on the north wall between the windows. The top portion contains a rare example of églomisé painting—reverse painting on glass—of an American eagle bearing in its talons the motto from the Great Seal of the United States. The looking glass, made in New York in the early 19th century, has an architectural frame of gilded wood. Below the looking glass is one of a pair of Phyfe caned settees. The other settee, flanked by sewing or work tables, stands against the south wall opposite the windows. In front of the windows are two of six matching Phyfe cross-bannister chairs with caned seats covered by cushions. The drum table in the center of the room is also attributed to Phyfe.

On the west wall is a neoclassical mantel from a house in Salem, Massachusetts. It dates from the early 19th century and is decorated with grape-leaf swags and bellflower pendants. To the right of the fireplace is a Sheraton-style armchair made in Portsmouth, New Hampshire; to the left is a Lannuier armchair matching the side chairs flanking the east door. This set is finely carved in leaf and rosette motifs.

On the mantel rests a pair of English silver-plate Argand lamps, a gift of the Marquis de Lafayette to Gen. Henry Knox, Secretary of War in Washington's Cabinet. Such lamps, named after their Swiss inventor, Aimé Argand, were a major innovation; George Washington ordered some in 1790, noting that by report they "consume their own smoke . . . give more light, and are cheaper than candles."

One of the many Athenaeum portraits of George Washington by Gilbert Stuart hangs over the mantel. Stuart painted three portraits of Washington from life, the Vaughan portrait (1795), now in the National Gallery of Art; the full-length Lansdowne portrait (1796), owned by the Earl of Rosebery and on loan to the National Portrait Gallery; and the Athenaeum portrait (1796), which was acquired by the Boston Athenaeum in 1876 and is now owned jointly by the National Portrait Gallery

THE LIBRARY

The lighthouse clock, patented in 1822 by Simon Willard of Roxbury, Massachusetts, has a fragile glass dome with an alarm bell inside. The medallion on the mahogany base shows the Marquis de Lafayette. Below: an Argand lamp presented by Lafayette to Gen. Henry Knox, his friend and comrade-in-arms.

and the Museum of Fine Arts in Boston. Gilbert Stuart kept the Athenaeum portrait throughout his life and made well over 50 replicas of it for patriotic Americans. The portrait in the Library was painted for a Baltimore family and, like all the copies, varies slightly from the original. Stuart also made copies of the Lansdowne portrait, one of which hangs in the East Room.

One of the bookshelves displays an unusual lighthouse clock made by Simon Willard to commemorate the visit of the Marquis de Lafayette to the United States in 1824-25. A likeness of Lafayette appears in a medallion on its base. Hanging in the corner of the room is a long wooden pole that unfolds to form a narrow ladder. Such ladders were often used in England as library steps; the one in this room is a reproduction of an 18th-century version. Called "machan" or "howdah" ladders, they were used in India for entering hunting blinds or for mounting and dismounting elephants.

Four portraits of American Indians by Charles Bird King flank the east door, and a fifth hangs over the entrance to the corridor. The paintings, given to the White House in 1962, are King's own copies from a set of eight portraits commissioned in 1821 for the American Indian archives, then located in Georgetown. In 1865, the originals—by that time in the Smithsonian Institution—were destroyed by fire.

The federal government, fearing that the powerful and militant tribes of the Great Plains would oppose westward expansion, invited a number of Indian leaders to visit the nation's most important cities and forts and to meet their "Great Father," the President. Government officials hoped to overawe these Indians with an impressive show of military strength, luxurious gifts, and elaborate ceremony.

When the Indians arrived in Washington, merchants fitted them out in military finery for an audience with President James Monroe. They were formally received by the President in the Red Room on February 4, 1822. With the help of interpreters, he thanked them for coming, spoke of the white man's strength and the blessings of peace, and offered to send missionaries to instruct them in Christianity and agriculture. The chiefs, impressed but feeling ill at ease in their new clothes, gravely replied that they admired the things they had seen but preferred their own life of trapping beaver and hunting buffalo. Sharitarish, their leader, added: " . . . we have plenty of land, if you will keep your people off it."

Each speaker laid a gift at the President's feet: moccasins, feathered headdresses, buffalo robes, and peace pipes. Before the party moved to the Blue Room for cake and wine, Sharitarish expressed the hope that Monroe would order the presents kept "in some conspicuous part of your lodge, so that when we are gone . . . if our children should visit this place, as we do now, they may see and recognize with pleasure the deposits of their fathers, and reflect on the times that are past." The gifts were unfortunately lost long ago, and efforts to avoid fighting the Great Plains tribes were unsuccessful.

THE VERMEIL ROOM

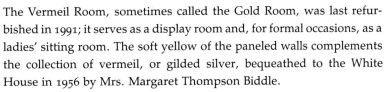

Douglas Chandor caught vivaciousness and changing moods in this multiple-image portrait of Eleanor Roosevelt, painted in his studio in New York City in 1949. A vermeil wine cooler (far left), made in London in 1823 by Philip Rundell, has as its handles classical figures reaching for grapes from an arbor.

The Vermeil Room, sometimes called the Gold Room, was last refurbished in 1991; it serves as a display room and, for formal occasions, as a ladies' sitting room. The soft yellow of the paneled walls complements the collection of vermeil, or gilded silver, bequeathed to the White House in 1956 by Mrs. Margaret Thompson Biddle.

The vermeil collection contains pieces from different services and includes the work of English Regency silversmith Paul Storr (1771-1844) and French Empire silversmith Jean-Baptiste-Claude Odiot (1763-1850). Pieces from the collection are used throughout the house and for some formal entertaining.

The green satin draperies are of early 19th-century design. The carpet is a Turkish Hereke of about 1860, chosen for its pale green background and gold silk highlights. In the center of the room stands a circular mahogany table made in the Empire Revival style later in the 19th century. Its tilt top is veneered in 12 wedge-shaped sections, each inlaid with a brass star. Hanging above it is a cut-glass chandelier with ten arms, which was made in England about 1785.

The French neoclassical mantel, dating from about 1830, was installed in 1962. It features two draped female figures in deep relief, which were derived from the work of Antonio Canova. Above the mantel is Elizabeth Shoumatoff's painting of Claudia (Lady Bird) Johnson. Mrs. Johnson chose the Jefferson Memorial, one of her favorite views, as the background for the picture, which was painted in the White House.

Portraits of three other First Ladies are exhibited in the Vermeil Room. On the south wall is a full-length portrait of Jacqueline Kennedy Onassis painted by Aaron Shikler in 1970; her New York apartment provided its background. On the east wall hang likenesses of Patricia Ryan Nixon by Henriette Wyeth and Anna Eleanor Roosevelt by Douglas Chandor. The latter, painted in 1949, conveys the subject's many moods and boundless energy and is inscribed by her in the upper right corner: "A trial made pleasant by the painter. Eleanor Roosevelt."

Against the south wall is a New York sofa dated 1800-10. It bears a straight crest rail with a sunburst-and-fan center tablet and reeded front legs. On either side stand Boston work tables made in the early 1800's and thought to be the work of either John or Thomas Seymour. Although not a pair, each has two drawers and a sewing-bag slide.

Placed along the north wall is a classical mahogany pier table with a marble top and gilded bronze caryatid heads and feet on reeded supports. It was made about 1805 in New York and is one of two tables in the room that bear the label of New York cabinetmaker Charles-Honoré Lannuier. He is also represented by three other tables in the room.

THE CHINA ROOM

The "Presidential Collection Room," now the China Room, was designated by Mrs. Woodrow Wilson in 1917 to display the growing collection of White House china. The room was redecorated in 1970, retaining the traditional red color scheme determined by the portrait of Mrs. Calvin Coolidge—painted by Howard Chandler Christy in 1924. President Coolidge, who was scheduled to sit for Christy, was too occupied that day with events concerning the Teapot Dome oil scandal. So the President postponed his appointment, and Mrs. Coolidge posed instead. The

red theme continues in the velvet-lined cabinets, silk taffeta draperies,
and the early 20th-century Indo-Ispahan rug. The cut-glass
chandelier, made about 1800, is in the English Regency style.
Flanking the portrait are two American chairs, called "Martha
Washington" or "lolling" chairs, made in the early 19th century.
The painting above the mantel, "View on the Mississippi Fifty-Seven
Miles Below St. Anthony Falls, Minneapolis," was completed by
Ferdinand Richardt in 1858—the year Minnesota achieved statehood.

Almost every past President is represented in the China Room either by state or family china or glassware. The collection is arranged chronologically, beginning to the right of the fireplace.

Even the earliest Presidents received government funds to purchase state china. However, by a special clause in the appropriation bills, "decayed furnishings" could be sold and the proceeds used to buy replacements. Such "furnishings" included state china, and during the 19th century the cupboards were frequently swept clean and the contents carted off to auction. The money could then be used to order a new china service that better suited the President and his family. Much china, deemed unusable because of cracks or other damage, was given away. Large amounts were also lost through breakage. Thousands of dollars' worth of china and glass were broken at the celebration following Andrew Jackson's inauguration, for example. Unruly crowds thronged the White House trying to catch a glimpse of the new President, who was finally forced to escape and spend the night at a boardinghouse.

Obviously, not much historical importance was attached to White House china during the first hundred years of the Presidency. In 1889, however, Mrs. Benjamin Harrison started to collect pieces from previous administrations, and her project was continued by Mrs. William McKinley. The collection was greatly expanded by Mrs. Theodore Roosevelt, who strongly opposed the sale of any White House china. She also stopped the practice of giving away or selling damaged china; it was broken and scattered into the Potomac River instead.

Many Presidents have chosen not to order new state china, either because it was not needed or because the appropriation was used for other things. Presidents who use their personal china in the White House take it with them when they leave; most of such pieces in the collection have been acquired from their descendants.

Until the administration of Woodrow Wilson all Presidential china was produced outside the United States—usually in France or England. Patriotic symbols, especially the American eagle, frequently appear in the china designs. The service chosen by Mrs. Lyndon B. Johnson also features American wildflowers. A new state china pattern selected by Mrs. Ronald Reagan was donated to the White House in 1982; a wide red border overlaid with gold latticework and edged with gold decorates the service plates.

For unabashed assertion of national pride, no china could outshine the exuberant Hayes service; ordered in 1879, it portrays American flora and fauna. The game platter with a strutting wild turkey is one of a series of painted and sculpted plates decorated with wild animals, fish, fruits, and vegetables. When the china first appeared at a state dinner, according to one report, it formed "the most conspicuous part of the furniture of the table."

Above: a serving platter from the flamboyant Hayes china, made in France by Haviland & Co. Early Presidential family china (bottom right): a Sèvres tureen owned by John and Abigail Adams; a Chinese export porcelain sugar bowl from Martha Washington's monogrammed personal china; a French cup and saucer, part of a service purchased by James Madison from James Monroe. Dolley Madison designed the monogram.

Below: plates from four state services. The Lyndon B. Johnson china, made by Castleton China, Inc., of Pennsylvania, features a border of flowers and an American eagle derived from the one on an amaranth-rimmed plate from the Monroe service, made in France by Dagoty et Honoré. Bordered in navy and gold, the Wilson china, ordered from Lenox of New Jersey, was the first state service made in the United States. The Reagan service also came from Lenox; an etched gold band and red border overlaid by gold latticework surround an ivory center with a raised gold Presidential seal.

Above: Classical figures adorn a rococo-revival punch bowl from Franklin Pierce's Administration. Mrs. Benjamin Harrison found the bowl in the White House attic and had it mended and put on display as an historical piece of White House china.

THE
DIPLOMATIC
RECEPTION
ROOM

The Diplomatic Reception Room serves as an entrance to the White House from the South Grounds for the family and for ambassadors arriving to present their credentials to the President. In the past the area has had diverse uses: as a boiler and furnace room and as the site of President Franklin D. Roosevelt's fireside chats.

Since 1960, the room has been furnished as a drawing room of the Federal period (1790-1820)—with many fine examples of the craftsmanship of New York and New England cabinetmakers. The gold-and-white color scheme was chosen at that time. A Regency chandelier of cut glass and gilt bronze was added in 1971. The current rug, installed in 1983, was woven specially for the room. Its border incorporates emblems of the 50 states.

The striking panoramic wallpaper in this room, "Views of North America," was first printed in 1834 by Jean Zuber et Cie in Rixheim, Alsace. (Wallpaper was widely used in 19th-century America and covered many of the White House walls at that time.) The complete set of 32 somewhat fanciful scenes, based on engravings of the 1820's, shows American landscapes that were particularly admired by Europeans. Starting to the left of the doorway from the Ground Floor Corridor are the Natural Bridge of Virginia, Niagara Falls, New York Bay, West Point, and Boston Harbor. Wooden blocks were used to print on panels composed of small sheets of paper.

The handsome, mahogany bookcase-desk on the west wall was made in Annapolis in 1797 and bears the label of John Shaw. The side chair at the desk, with splats forming Gothic arches, is one of a pair made in New York about 1800. It matches the two settees that flank the desk and a pair of armchairs. All six pieces are attributed to the New York workshop of Abraham Slover and Jacob Taylor.

A patriotic eagle motif in wood inlay decorates the bonnet of the mahogany tall case clock with musical chimes. Its works were made by Effingham Embree of New York.

Made about 1800, the American lolling chairs are not a pair: One, with Hepplewhite-style straight, square front legs, was made in New York; the other, with Sheraton-style turned legs, may have come from Massachusetts. Also in the room are other American pieces made between 1790 and 1800: two wing chairs, a bowed-back sofa made in New York, and a pair of Philadelphia side chairs.

One of the three oval rooms in the White House proper, the Diplomatic Reception Room exhibits American Federal-period furniture. The room provides a handsome entrance for diplomats arriving to present credentials.

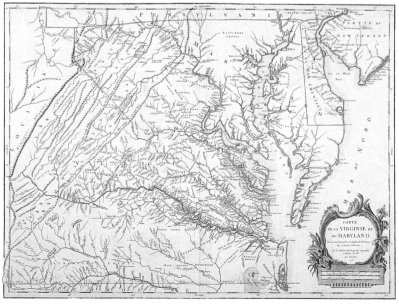

THE MAP ROOM

Chippendale-style furniture and a 19th-century Kirman rug decorate the Map Room. Left: Rare 1755 French version of a map charted by colonial surveyors Joshua Fry and Peter Jefferson (Thomas Jefferson's father) hangs on the east wall, covering a case of world maps presented by the National Geographic Society.

The Map Room, used by President Franklin D. Roosevelt as a situation room from which to follow the course of World War II, now serves as a private meeting room for the President or the First Lady. It was decorated in 1970, and again in 1994, as a sitting room in the Chippendale style, which flourished in America during the last half of the 18th century.

Named after the English furniture designer Thomas Chippendale, this style combines the graceful lines of Queen Anne furniture with carved motifs in more elaborate rococo, Gothic, and Chinese styles. The handsome, walnut high chest of drawers on the south wall was made in Philadelphia about 1770 and has shell carvings on its pediment and apron and the knees of its cabriole legs. The side chairs that flank the high chest, from a set of four and an armchair, were made about 1770 in Philadelphia, possibly by Thomas Affleck. Attributed to the same cabinetmaker is the mahogany easy chair with square, upholstered back.

To the right of the window is a blockfront desk made between 1760 and 1780. Cabinetmakers in Massachusetts and Rhode Island adapted the Chippendale style to this uniquely American design, in which the center of three vertical panels is recessed. Above the desk hangs John Wesley Jarvis's 1817 portrait of Andrew Jackson, based on a painting by Nathan W. Wheeler, a veteran of the Battle of New Orleans.

The simple sandstone mantel was made from stone removed during the Truman renovation of the White House. Above it hangs the last situation map prepared in this room for President Roosevelt, on April 3, 1945. To the right of the fireplace is a chest of drawers with a serpentine front made in Philadelphia about 1765. On it rests a medicine chest that is believed to have belonged to President and Mrs. James Madison and to have been taken from the White House just before the building was burned during the War of 1812.

Above the chest of drawers is a portrait of Benjamin Henry Latrobe painted by Charles Willson Peale about 1804—at the time Latrobe was appointed Surveyor of the Public Buildings by President Thomas Jefferson. The artist was the patriarch of a family of painters. Displayed on the north wall is a still life by his brother James Peale and another based on one of James's works by Charles's third son, Rubens Peale.

On the east wall hangs "The Mellow Autumn Time," a landscape by Jasper Cropsey, a member of the Hudson River School. In front of the Chippendale-style sofa below it stands a tea table with a gadrooned apron edge and cabriole legs made between 1760 and 1780 in New York.

The 19th-century Kirman carpet features colored medallions on an ivory ground. An English cut-glass chandelier with star pendants, made around 1765, lights the room.

THE
NORTH
ENTRANCE

The large Entrance Hall and the Cross Hall formed part of James Hoban's original plans for the White House. The basic design has not been
altered, although modifications have been made during various renovations. During the 19th century two principal stairways led to the second
floor. The broad staircase at the west end of the Cross Hall (see page
145) was removed in 1902 to increase the size of the State Dining Room.
At the same time, the remaining stairway, opening into the Cross Hall,
was enlarged. During the 1948-52 renovation, this stairway was repositioned to open into the Entrance Hall.

The Cross Hall, with marble walls and floors added during the Truman renovation, is lighted by two Adam-style cut-glass chandeliers
made in London about 1790. The bronze light standards date from the
Roosevelt renovation of 1902 as does the design of the decorative plaster
ceiling. An Italian settee with an eagle decoration stands beneath the
1967 portrait of Dwight D. Eisenhower by J. Anthony Wills.

Other Presidential portraits hang at the east end of the Cross Hall:
Lyndon B. Johnson by Elizabeth Shoumatoff, Gerald R. Ford by Everett
Raymond Kinstler, and Jimmy Carter by Herbert E. Abrams. A portrait
of President Kennedy painted by Aaron Shikler hangs at the west end of
the hall. Two marble busts are displayed in niches along the south wall:
American diplomat and poet Joel Barlow by Jean-Antoine Houdon and
George Washington after Houdon.

The Cross Hall has not always had this look of elegant simplicity. In
1865 an inventory dismissed its furnishings as "all pretty common."
Perhaps its most spectacular alteration occurred in 1882 when President
Arthur called on Louis C. Tiffany of New York to redecorate the mansion. A stained-glass screen, reaching from floor to ceiling, was placed
between the columns to divide the Cross Hall from the Entrance Hall
(see pages 130-31). One observer remarked: "The light coming through
the partition of wrinkled stained glass mosaic makes a marvelously rich
and gorgeous effect, falling upon the gilded niches where stand dwarf
palmetto trees, the silvery network of the ceiling, and the sumptuous
furniture. . . ." In these lavish surroundings the Grover Clevelands held
their last dinner for the Diplomatic Corps, by then far too large for the
State Dining Room. The McKinleys also gave dinners here. Apparently,
the Tiffany screen did not block the flow of cold air from the North Entrance very effectively: "A gale roared through the improvised banquet
hall whenever the front door was opened," writes historian Margaret
Leech, "and the floor was so cold that the divans were robbed of cushions to make footstools for the ladies."

Until 1902, when the President's second-floor offices were moved to

*The Cross Hall (above),
separated from the
Entrance Hall by the
colonnade constructed
after Hoban's original
design, extends between
the State Dining Room
and the East Room.
A 1991 portrait of
Ronald W. Reagan
(opposite), by Everett
Raymond Kinstler,
hangs in the Grand
Staircase. A marble bust
of American diplomat
and poet Joel Barlow,
by Jean-Antoine Houdon,
(opposite, right) is
displayed in a niche
beyond the flags.*

The portrait of Gerald R. Ford, by Everett Raymond Kinstler, hangs at the east end of the Cross Hall. President Ford sat for the painting in his home in Vail, Colorado, in July 1977, six months after he left office.

Herbert E. Abrams painted the portrait of Jimmy Carter in Plains, Georgia, in 1982. Displayed in the Cross Hall, it depicts Carter seated in an armchair from the Red Room.

THE NORTH ENTRANCE

Presidential portraits, a cut-glass chandelier, and red carpet on marble steps decorate the Grand Staircase, the elegant passage between the Family and State Floors. On state occasions the President and First Lady usually escort official visitors down this stairway to the Entrance Hall, where they pose for photographers.

the newly built West Wing, the Entrance Hall served as a reception area and as a busy passageway. The furnishings were, by necessity, utilitarian and, judging from the inventories, consistently worn.

The Entrance Hall is seen by visitors as they leave the White House. It is set off from the Cross Hall by the Hoban-designed colonnade and is decorated in the same style. Its furnishings include a French pier table purchased by Monroe in 1817 and a pair of French settees with carved mahogany swans' heads. A suite of early 19th-century Italian gilded furniture in the Empire style was placed in the halls in 1973. Frank O. Salisbury's portrait of Franklin D. Roosevelt hangs in the Entrance Hall, as does Martha Greta Kempton's painting of Harry S. Truman.

The Grand Staircase is often used on ceremonial occasions. Before state dinners, the President greets his guests of honor in the Yellow Oval Room; then they descend the stairs to the East Room where the other guests are gathered. Along the stairway hang portraits of 20th-century Presidents, including Ronald W. Reagan by Everett Raymond Kinstler, Richard M. Nixon by J. Anthony Wills, Herbert Hoover by Elmer W. Greene, and Warren G. Harding by F. Luis Mora; a portrait of Mrs. William Howard Taft by Bror Kronstrand is also in the stairway. Above the American pier table on the landing is F. Graham Cootes's painting of Woodrow Wilson. An English cut-glass chandelier from the mid-19th century lights the stairway at the first landing.

THE EAST ROOM

The East Room, scene of many historic White House events, was designated by Hoban as the "Public Audience Room." It normally contains little furniture and traditionally is used for large gatherings, such as dances, after-dinner entertainments, concerts, weddings, funerals, award presentations, press conferences, and bill-signing ceremonies.

Today the East Room retains the late 18th-century classical style to which it was restored by architects McKim, Mead & White during the Roosevelt renovation of 1902. An oak floor of Fontainebleau parquetry was installed at that time as were the bronze electric-light standards, upholstered benches, and three Bohemian cut-glass chandeliers. The walls were paneled in wood with classical fluted pilasters and relief insets. The paneling was painted white, and delicate plaster decoration was added to the ceiling.

The room was originally designed with two fireplaces in the west wall and five windows in the east wall. Latrobe's 1807 plan to wall in four of the windows was adopted in the first quarter of the 19th century, and two new fireplaces were added. New marble mantels were installed over the four fireplaces during the Truman renovation of 1948-52. A gold-and-white color scheme was chosen by Mrs. Theodore Roosevelt, although Charles McKim originally had envisioned crimson draperies for this room. Red draperies were substituted during the Franklin D. Roosevelt Administration, but the Truman renovation returned the East Room to the gold-and-white theme. The gold damask draperies of French fabric now at the windows were hung in 1983.

The Steinway grand piano with gilt American eagle supports was designed by Eric Gugler and was given to the White House in 1938 by the manufacturer. It is decorated with gilt stenciling by Dunbar Beck.

The full-length portrait of George Washington that hangs here is one of several replicas made by Gilbert Stuart of his "Lansdowne" portrait. It is the only object known to have remained in the White House since 1800—except for periods of reconstruction, such as after the British burned the mansion during the War of 1812.

Dolley Madison had refused to abandon the portrait as she fled; she wrote to her sister on the day of the fire: "Our kind friend, Mr. Carroll, has come to hasten my departure, and is in a very bad humor with me because I insist on waiting until the large picture of Gen. Washington is

The East Room, largest and most formal of the state reception rooms, was not finished until 1829. The present classical decor dates largely from the 1902 renovation. On the east wall hang a Gilbert Stuart portrait of George Washington and John Singer Sargent's 1903 portrait of Theodore Roosevelt.

secured, and it requires to be unscrewed from the wall. This process was found too tedious for these perilous moments; I have ordered the frame to be broken, and the canvas taken out; it is done,—and the precious portrait placed in the hands of two gentlemen of New York, for safe keeping. And now, dear sister, I must leave this house, or the retreating army will make me a prisoner in it, by filling up the road I am directed to take. . . ." Her efforts were successful, and the portrait was returned to the White House when the rebuilding was completed. The companion portrait of Martha Washington was painted by Eliphalet F. Andrews in 1878.

Although intended by Hoban to be the most elegant of the state reception rooms, the East Room remained unfinished for 29 years. It was here that the John Adams family, first occupants of the White House, dried their laundry, presumably with the help of two "Ten Plate" stoves listed in an inventory of February 26, 1801.

Thomas Jefferson partitioned the space to create two rooms for his secretary, Meriwether Lewis—later co-leader of the Lewis and Clark expedition—who had to move his quarters when the East Room ceiling fell in. Architect Benjamin Latrobe, appointed by Jefferson as Surveyor of Public Buildings, noted on a floor plan executed in 1803: "Public Audience Chamber—entirely unfinished, the ceiling has given way." Jefferson's inventory of 1809 lists "34 armed Chairs black and Gold" in the "Large Unfinished Room," and "1 Table & Kettles for washing Tumblers," indicating that the room may have been used as a makeshift butler's pantry as well as a storage area. James Madison met with his Cabinet in the south end of the East Room; but whatever furnishings the room might have contained were destroyed in the fire of 1814, and no record of them remains.

This gilded bronze candelabra is one of four purchased in 1817 by President Monroe. Thought to be the work of French bronze caster Pierre-Philippe Thomire, they are displayed on the mantels on the west wall.

After the fire, restoration of the White House included work on the "principal drawing room"; by November 21, 1818, Hoban reported that the floor had been laid, the walls and ceiling plastered, and the cornice, frieze, architrave, and decorative woodwork nearly finished. The appropriations, however, were not adequate to furnish the East Room properly. Four sofas and two dozen chairs made by William King (see page 119) were placed in the room, but their upholstery was unfinished. They remained so when President John Quincy Adams opened the room to provide space for the large New Year's Day receptions during his term of office.

In 1829, President Andrew Jackson finally decorated the East Room in grand style, at a cost to the taxpayer of more than $9,000. The purchases Jackson made included "three 18-light" chandeliers with cut glass of "remarkable brilliancy," a "3-light centre lamp supported by female figures," eight "5-light" gilded wall brackets, and various table lamps. Four fireplaces were fitted with black marble mantels with "Italian black and gold fronts"; four huge gilt-frame mirrors were placed above these mantels. Almost 500 yards of red-bordered Brussels carpet was purchased for the floor, and lemon-yellow paper covered the walls.

A clergyman from New England found this "great levee apartment . . . truly magnificent," carefully noting the "light-blue satin-silk" on the sofas and chairs and the "white, blue, and light-yellow commingled" hues of the curtains. Even if the ladies of his party agreed that the rich carpet "needed the cleansing effect of tea-leaves," he concluded that: "On the whole it is a seat worthy of the people's idol."

During the Civil War years and the administration of Abraham Lincoln there was much activity in the East Room. At one time during the war Union troops occupied the room. In 1864 the East Room was the scene of a large reception given by President Lincoln in honor of Ulysses S. Grant shortly before his appointment as head of all the Union armies. In April of 1865 the East Room was again filled with people, but this time they were mourners surrounding the body of President Lincoln after he had been assassinated by John Wilkes Booth. Lincoln lay in state on a black-draped catafalque, much as he had foreseen in a dream a few weeks earlier. Seven Presidents have lain in state in the East Room, including John F. Kennedy in November 1963.

Furnishings in the East Room had become shabby and worn by the time General Grant became President. In 1873 a drastic renovation transformed the room into a salon decorated in the Victorian style (see page 124). The ceiling was divided into three sections with ornate false beams supported by gilded columns. Large gas chandeliers, patterned carpeting and wall coverings, heavy mirrors, and rich fabrics created what sometimes has been referred to as "steamboat palace" decor. In this setting President Grant's daughter, Nellie, was married in 1874 under a huge bell of roses. An elaborate wedding breakfast followed in the State Dining Room. The next wedding to take place in the East Room was that of Alice Roosevelt in 1906. By that time, the room had been restored to the classic simplicity of the late 18th century. The most recent wedding here was Lynda Johnson's in 1967.

Gilbert Stuart's 1797 portrait of George Washington was rescued by Dolley Madison shortly before the British burned the White House on August 24, 1814. The painting has been the property of the mansion since 1800.

When President Arthur redecorated the White House in 1882, Louis C. Tiffany found it necessary only to install silver paper on the ceiling of the East Room and to increase the number of potted plants. All of these heavy Victorian adornments were swept away in the 1902 restoration. During the Theodore Roosevelt Administration, this room became the scene of some rather unusual activities, including a wrestling match arranged to entertain some 50 to 60 guests of the President. The exuberant Roosevelt children are also known to have used the East Room for roller-skating.

THE GREEN ROOM

Although intended by Hoban to be the "Common Dining Room," the Green Room has served many purposes since the White House was first occupied in 1800. The inventory of February 1801 indicates that it was first used as a "Lodging Room." Thomas Jefferson, the second occupant of the White House, used it as a dining room with a "canvass floor cloth, painted Green," foreshadowing the present color scheme. James Madison made it a sitting room since his Cabinet met in the East Room next door, and the Monroes used it as the "Card Room" with two tables for the whist players among their guests.

When the Monroes, the first occupants of the White House after the fire of 1814, set about refurnishing the mansion, they decorated the room with green silks. With the next President, John Quincy Adams, came the name "Green Drawing Room"; and a green drawing room it has remained, traditionally serving as a parlor for small teas and receptions and on occasion for formal dinners.

Not every President has chosen a green everyone liked. The shade that Andrew Jackson approved provoked unfavorable comment from the ladies; they found the color "odious . . . from the sallow look it imparts." Styles in the room changed as frequently as the tastes of the Presidents until the time of Theodore Roosevelt, when it was furnished with reproductions of early 19th-century American furniture. Not until the Coolidge Administration, however, was authentic Federal-period furniture placed in the room.

The Green Room was completely refurbished in 1971. Its walls were re-covered with the delicate green watered-silk fabric originally chosen by Mrs. Kennedy in 1962. Draperies of striped beige, green, and coral satin—a major part of the 1971 renovation—were carefully designed from a pattern shown in an early 19th-century periodical. The coral-and-gilt ornamental cornices are surmounted by a pair of hand-carved, gilded American eagles with outspread wings. The eagle, patriotic symbol of the United States, was one of the favored decorative motifs of the Federal period and appears in many forms in this room.

The carpet is a copy of a Turkish Hereke of 19th-century design, with a multicolored pattern on a green field. This green background, sometimes found in small Muslim prayer rugs, is unusual in a rug this large. The cut-glass-and-ormolu chandelier, made in France in the early 19th century, was installed in the room in 1975.

The Green Room, a first-floor parlor, was completely refurbished in 1971. Its furniture, in the styles of the Federal period, includes many pieces attributed to the famous New York cabinetmaker Duncan Phyfe.

As wife of the Secretary of State, Louisa Catherine Adams began posing for Gilbert Stuart in 1821; this portrait was not completed until five years later when her husband, John Quincy Adams, was President. David Martin's 1767 portrait of a scholarly, aging Benjamin Franklin hangs over the mantel. "Farmyard in Winter" (below), painted by George H. Durrie in 1858, shows nostalgia for an idealized past. The unusual work table (right), one of two flanking the fireplace, has a hinged lid and sides that open to reveal trays and small compartments. It may have been designed for fine sewing or possibly for painting miniatures. The

Argand lamp, named after its Swiss inventor Aimé Argand, was ingeniously designed with a tubular wick to burn brighter and cleaner than other lamps of the late 18th century.

In "a noble, or genteel house," wrote Thomas Sheraton, the English furniture designer, a drawing room "should possess all the elegance embellishments can give." Most of the furnishings now in the Green Room date from the years 1800-15, the period of Sheraton's greatest influence on American decor. Many of the pieces are attributed to the New York workshop of the well-known Scottish-born cabinetmaker Duncan Phyfe, who enjoyed a reputation for fine design and excellence of craftsmanship.

Among the pieces attributed to the Phyfe workshop is the Sheraton bookcase-desk standing between the windows on the south wall. The desk has many details of Phyfe's work, including the richly figured mahogany veneers that contrast with the satinwood-faced drawers and pigeonholes inside its cylinder section. Its shelves display early 19th-century Chinese export porcelain and a pair of unusual vases made by Tucker & Hemphill of Philadelphia. The manufacturers decorated the pieces with portraits of Andrew Jackson and the Marquis de Lafayette and the American eagle bearing a flag. Above the desk hangs "Lighter Relieving a Steamboat Aground," painted by George Caleb Bingham in 1847, after he returned to Missouri from the East Coast and began depicting scenes of a lifestyle that was fast disappearing.

The New York armchair at the desk bears the signature of Lawrence Ackerman, one of Phyfe's upholsterers, on the seat frame. In the window niches stands a pair of rare mahogany Duncan Phyfe benches with reeded edges and rolled arms, made for a New York family about 1810 and also upholstered by Ackerman.

The neoclassical marble mantel on the east wall is one of a pair ordered by Monroe in 1817 and installed in the State Dining Room. During the Roosevelt renovation of 1902, this one was placed here and the other in the Red Room. A French bronze-doré clock made by Robert Robin (1742-1799), clockmaker to Louis XV and Louis XVI, sits on the mantel. Above the mantel hangs a life portrait of Benjamin Franklin painted in London in 1767 by Scottish artist David Martin.

On each side of the fireplace are two almost identical and exceedingly rare mahogany work tables ingeniously designed with hidden compartments. Attributed to the New York workshop of Duncan Phyfe, they were probably made about 1810. A pair of Sheffield Argand lamps with oval-back mirrors, made in England in the early 19th century, stands on the work tables.

The carved-and-reeded mahogany pole screen to the left of the fireplace is a fine example of the New York Regency style from the Federal period. The elliptical embroidered-silk screen features the symbolic figure of Hope surrounded by a floral border.

Of particular note are the two upholstered Sheraton-style chairs that flank the fireplace. The New York wing chair on the left dates from about 1800. The armchair on the right is inscribed: "This frame made by D. Phyfe/ for Mr. Van Rensellaer [sic] Albany/ Stuffed by L. Ackerman New York 1811."

Doors on either side of the fireplace open to the East Room. Above the left door is an 1858 portrait of James K. Polk, one in the series of Presidential portraits painted by George P. A. Healy. Above the right door is a portrait of Benjamin Harrison, which was painted in 1895 by Eastman Johnson.

On the north wall, opposite the windows, are portraits by Gilbert Stuart of John Quincy Adams, painted in 1818, and his wife, Louisa. The paintings remained in the Adams family until a great-great-grandson, also named John Quincy Adams, presented them to the White House in 1970 and 1971.

American paintings of later periods are also displayed on the north wall. Below the portrait of Mrs. Adams hangs "Farmyard in Winter," which was painted by George H. Durrie in 1858 and shows an idyllic Connecticut farm; below the portrait of President Adams is "The Mosquito Net," painted in 1912 by John Singer Sargent and kept in his own collection. Above the door leading to the Cross Hall is "Niagara Falls," completed between 1852 and 1854 by Hudson River School artist John Frederick Kensett.

Identical mahogany pedestal pier tables of exceptional quality, made about 1815 in the workshop of Duncan Phyfe, stand beneath the paintings on the north wall. The cloverleaf tops are carved from King of Prussia marble quarried near Philadelphia. Possibly made as a pair, they were given to the White House by different donors.

The distinctive oval design, chosen by John Frederick Kensett for this view of Niagara Falls, echoes the curve of the falls itself. America's natural beauties, and Niagara Falls in particular, were popular subjects for landscape painters in the 19th century. Kensett made lengthy trips from his New York City home to paint the mountains of New York and New England.

On the west wall hangs "The Indian's Vespers," painted in 1847 by Asher B. Durand, a well-known American landscape painter. Below it hangs an historically important 19th-century American cityscape "Independence Hall in Philadelphia," painted by Ferdinand Richardt in the period 1858-63. The painting was found in India, restored, and given to the White House in 1963. On each side of this painting are matching mahogany-and-gilt mirrored wall sconces dating from about 1800.

Below these paintings is a handsome Duncan Phyfe settee of about 1810 that bears trademarks of his work—the tied reeds and clustered wheatears carved on the crest rail, the outcurved arms, and the reeded legs and seat rail. Cluster-columned drop-leaf library tables on either side of the settee are also attributed to Phyfe's workshop.

In front of the settee is a New York sofa table with unusual cloverleaf drop ends. The two Sheraton mahogany side chairs near it, probably made in Philadelphia about 1810, are rare for the period because of the upholstered backs, which indicate that they were originally intended for use in a drawing room. (Typical Sheraton open-back chairs could also be used in a dining room.)

On the sofa table are several historic pieces of Presidential silver, the most important being a Sheffield coffee urn of about 1785 that belonged to John Adams. It was considered by President Adams to be among his "most prized possessions." An engraved, ribbon-hung ellipse above the spigot bears the initials "JAA," for John and Abigail Adams. The matching French candlesticks that flank the urn were bought by James Madison from James Monroe in 1803 and appear in subsequent inventories of the Madisons' household furnishings.

Portraits of two Presidents hang above the doors on the west wall. Ralph E. W. Earl depicted Andrew Jackson (see page 120) in the White House about 1835, while Jackson was President; James Reid Lambdin painted William Henry Harrison in Ohio in 1835.

"Lighter Relieving a Steamboat Aground," painted by George Caleb Bingham in 1847, hangs above the secretary in the Green Room. This genre scene portrays flatboatmen along the Mississippi or the Missouri River. Paintings on the west wall (right) depict both wilderness and city scenes of America in the mid-19th century: Asher B. Durand's "The Indian's Vespers" and, below it, "Independence Hall in Philadelphia" by Ferdinand Richardt.

THE BLUE ROOM

Elegant after a 1995 refurbishing, the oval Blue Room contains many furnishings in the French Empire style—the decor chosen for the room by President James Monroe in 1817. A settee and seven of the original gilded chairs fashioned for Monroe by Parisian cabinetmaker Pierre-Antoine Bellangé form the nucleus of the present furnishings. The Empire style originated in France during Napoleon's reign and is characterized by richly carved rectilinear furniture based on Greek, Roman, and Egyptian forms. Typical decorative motifs evident in the Blue Room include acanthus foliage, imperial eagles, wreaths, urns, stars, and classical figures. Swags and brass mountings were often used in drapery designs.

The "elliptic saloon," with the Yellow Oval Room above and the Diplomatic Reception Room below it, formed the most elegant architectural feature of Hoban's plans for the White House. For the south wall of the Blue Room, he designed French doors flanked by long windows. An oval portico with curving stairs was included in these original plans but was not built until 1824.

The Blue Room has always been used as a reception room except for a brief period during the administration of John Adams when it served as a south entrance hall. During the Madison Administration, architect Benjamin Latrobe designed a suite of classical-revival furniture for the room, but only some working drawings remain (see pages 112-13); the furnishings were destroyed in the fire of 1814.

When President Monroe redecorated the "large oval room" after the fire, he used the French Empire style. Monroe ordered a suite of French mahogany furniture through the American firm Russell and La Farge, with offices in Le Havre, France. However, the firm shipped gilded furniture instead, asserting that "mahogany is not generally admitted in the furniture of a Saloon, even at private gentlemen's houses." The order included a pier table; two large canapés, or sofas; 18 armchairs; two bergères, or armchairs with enclosed and upholstered sides, for the President and First Lady; 18 side chairs; four upholstered stools; and six footstools. Monroe's purchases for the Blue Room also included two large looking glasses; two screens; a bronze-doré clock; curtains that hung from arched gilt poles with eagles in the center; crimson flocked wallpaper; various lighting devices; ornaments in glass, porcelain, and bronze-doré; and an oval Aubusson rug, woven specially for this room and described in the bill of sale as green velvet with the national arms in the center. The furniture was decorated with carved sprigs of olive, although Monroe had asked for eagles. The upholstery fabric was listed as double-warp satin in delicate crimson and two shades of gold, with an American eagle woven into the center of a wreath of laurel.

The bill from Russell and La Farge described these and other articles as "for the Account and Risk" of the President. In fact, Monroe ran some political risk; there was considerable public pressure to buy only those goods made in the United States. William Lee, who was in charge of ordering the furniture, wrote somewhat defensively, "It must be acknowledged that the [French] articles are of the very first quality. . . ." Lee praised Bellangé's suite as "substantial heavy furniture, which should always remain in its place, and form, as it were, a part of the house; such as could be handed down through a succession of Presidents, suited to the dignity and character of the nation."

In 1837, President Van Buren redecorated the oval salon and started the tradition of a "blue room." In 1860, however, President Buchanan sold the Bellangé chairs and sofas at auction and replaced them with a Victorian rococo-revival suite (see pages 126-27); it served into the Theodore Roosevelt Administration. Some of Monroe's other purchases were retained, including the Bellangé pier table, a French clock, and

The Hannibal clock displayed on the mantel was the work of Denière and Matelin, noted French bronze casters who made many of the bronze-doré objects purchased in 1817 by President Monroe.

some of the ornaments. In the renovation of 1902, McKim, Mead & White restored the Empire decor and designed a set of furniture for the Blue Room based on the Bellangé originals. The walls were covered with a heavy, steel blue ribbed silk, woven to match a sample from the Napoleonic era. The new oak floor of herringbone parquet was uncarpeted.

Blue fabrics served as both wall coverings and draperies from 1902 until 1962, when the room was redecorated and the walls covered with cream-colored striped satin. By that time, the White House had been given three of the original Bellangé chairs, from which copies were made. A fourth of the original chairs was acquired in 1963.

In 1972 the room was completely redecorated again. Other Empire furnishings, including three more of the original Bellangé chairs, were added. One of the original Bellangé sofas, designed with a curved frame to fit the contours of the Blue Room, was acquired in 1978, restored, and placed here in 1981. The darker, sapphire blue silk upholstery fabric chosen for the 1995 refurbishing repeats the previous gold eagle medallion design that was derived from a chair depicted in John Vanderlyn's portrait of James Monroe (see page 116). The carpet was derived from an English design of 1815.

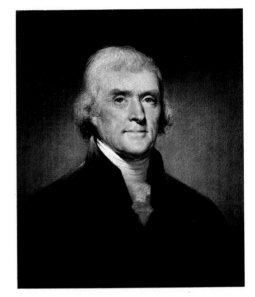

Thomas Jefferson as Vice President: an 1800 life portrait by Rembrandt Peale that was popularized by engravings.

The light gold wallpaper was adapted from an early-19th-century American paper, and the blue and gold borders were based on French papers from the same period. Sapphire satin draperies added in 1995 are trimmed with a blue and gold tape adapted from the wallpaper frieze.

The woodwork, painted white with a rubbed paint finish, and the gilding on the acanthus leaves in the cornice and in the ceiling medallion reflect the style of finish found in an American room in the first quarter of the 19th century.

The early 19th-century Empire chandelier, made in France of gilded wood and cut glass, is encircled by acanthus leaves. This motif also appears in the wallpaper borders, the cornice, and the oval plaster ceiling medallion above the chandelier.

To the left of the center window hangs John Vanderlyn's portrait of James Madison, commissioned in 1816 by James Monroe when he was President Madison's Secretary of State. To the right is a portrait of Thomas Jefferson by Rembrandt Peale, painted in Philadelphia in 1800, when Jefferson was Vice President. Jefferson was pleased with the painting, from which engravings were made.

On the west wall near the windows hangs a portrait of John Adams that was painted by John Trumbull about 1793, when Adams was Vice President. This painting—commissioned from the artist by John Jay, the first Chief Justice of the U. S. Supreme Court—is one of three similar portraits that Trumbull made of Adams.

Over the sofa is an 1859 portrait of John Tyler by George P. A. Healy;

it is considered to be the finest in the series of Presidential portraits Healy painted for the White House under a commission from Congress. Among the documents illustrated in the portrait is one pertaining to Texas, which, although annexed on March 3, 1845, was not admitted to the Union until December—nine months after Tyler left office.

The early 19th-century marble mantel on the east wall, acquired in 1972, is in the neoclassical style and is similar to the two Italian mantels purchased by Monroe. Above it is a New York Federal looking glass surmounted by a spread-wing American eagle. The precedent for such overmantel looking glasses in the Blue Room was set during the term of James Madison. The bronze-doré wall sconces hanging on either side of the looking glass were made in France about 1830.

One of the two Empire clocks purchased by Monroe is displayed on the mantel. Called the Hannibal clock, it bears a standing figure of the famous general from Carthage who led his troops, with some 40 elephants, across the Alps to fight the Romans in 218 B.C. The pair of French porcelain vases on the mantel were received by the Monroes in the same shipment as the Bellangé furniture. Each vase features a painted scene of Passy, the fashionable suburb of Paris where Benjamin Franklin lived while serving as American minister to France.

This Bellangé bergère— an armchair with closed and upholstered sides—was purchased in 1817 by James Monroe.

To the right of the mantel hangs a portrait of Elizabeth Kortright Monroe that is believed to have been painted by John Vanderlyn in 1816 or 1820. It is still owned by the Monroe family. On the other side of the mantel is a portrait of James Monroe by Samuel F. B. Morse. The artist and inventor visited the White House in 1819 while working on a full-length portrait of the President for the city of Charleston, South Carolina. This likeness is the bust-length life portrait ordered by the Monroe family at that time.

The mahogany marble-top table in the middle of the room has been in the White House since 1817, when it was purchased by President Monroe. Also in the room are two pier tables with mahogany columns and white marble tops; one was made around 1810 in France, and the other, labeled by Charles-Honore Lannuier, in New York around 1815.

Flanking the doorway to the Cross Hall are two scenes: "A View of Boston Harbor," painted in 1854 by Fitz Hugh Lane, on the left, and "Boys Crabbing," an 1855 oil by William Ranney, on the right. Above the doorway is Anders Zorn's 1911 portrait of William Howard Taft. The Swedish artist depicted the President in the Blue Room, seated on one of the 1902 armchairs.

Beneath the French gilded-wood chandelier stands a marble-top table that has been in the White House since it was purchased by President Monroe in 1817. George P. A. Healy's portrait of John Tyler hangs on the west wall above the Bellangé sofa.

THE
RED
ROOM

Furnished in the Empire style of 1810-30, the Red
Room—one of the four state reception rooms in the
White House—contains several pieces of furniture from
the New York workshop of the French-born cabinetmaker
Charles-Honoré Lannuier. An 1842 portrait by Henry
Inman of Angelica Singleton Van Buren, President Martin
Van Buren's daughter-in-law and official hostess, hangs
above the mantel. A white marble bust of Van Buren in
the neoclassical style appears in the portrait; it is one
of three busts of Van Buren executed by Hiram Powers,
for whom the President posed in 1836. One of these
busts is displayed on the wall between the windows.

Benjamin Latrobe's 1803 drawing of the State Floor indicates that the Red Room served as "the President's Antichamber" for the Cabinet Room or President's Library next door. During the Madison Administration the antechamber became the "Yellow Drawing Room" and the scene of Dolley Madison's fashionable Wednesday night receptions. In "that centre of attraction," said a lady who knew her well, one saw "all these whom fashion, fame, beauty, wealth or talents, have render'd celebrated." The room has usually served as a parlor or sitting room; recent Presidents have held small dinner parties here.

In 1971 the Red Room was redecorated, preserving the American Empire style chosen in 1962 during the John F. Kennedy Administration. The elegance of the Red Room furniture derives from a combination of richly carved and finished woods with ormolu mounts (decorative hardware made of gilded bronze) in characteristic designs such as dolphins, acanthus leaves, lions' heads, and sphinxes. The furniture displays many motifs similar to those of the French pieces now in the Blue Room. Egyptian motifs were extensively used in French Empire furnishings following Napoleon's 1798-99 campaign in Egypt, and many of these same designs were adopted by cabinetmakers working in New York, Boston, and Philadelphia.

The furniture in the Red Room dates from the years 1810-30. The rare mahogany secretary-bookcase between the windows is attributed to Charles-Honoré Lannuier and exhibits the characteristic Empire rectilinear shape and ornamental brass hardware. The lancet arches in its glazed doors are a Gothic motif. Also attributed to Lannuier is the mahogany sofa table to the left of the fireplace. It has gilt winged-caryatid supports and the paw feet commonly used in Empire furniture. Lannuier's labeled masterpiece, and the most important piece of American Empire furniture in the White House collection, is the marble-top gueridon, or small round table, opposite the fireplace. This table is made of mahogany and various fruitwoods with a trompe-l'oeil top of marble inlaid in a geometric pattern. Bronze-doré female heads surmount the delicately carved and reeded legs.

To the right of the fireplace is a graceful American Empire sofa with painted and gilded dolphin feet. The sofa has the distinctive Empire curved back rail and scrolled arms. Behind it is a New York Empire card table, one of three tables in the room with a carved lyre design. An ancient stringed musical instrument, the lyre was widely used in Empire furniture as a decorative motif for table supports and chair backs.

The bronze-doré clock on the mantel, made by the well-known Parisian bronze caster Pierre Joseph Gouthière, was given to the White House in 1952 by President Vincent Auriol of France. The clock was designed during the late 18th century to play pastoral music on a miniature organ inside the gilded case.

The early 19th-century French gilt porcelain vases on either side of the clock are decorated with likenesses of George Washington and the Marquis de Lafayette. To the right of the fireplace is an American

Empire music stand holding sheet music for a march entitled "President Jackson's Grand March."

During the 19th century the Red Room was often used as a music room where families gathered on Sunday evenings. The furnishings occasionally included a piano or other musical instruments, such as the pianoforte and guitar ordered by Dolley Madison.

All the fabrics now in the Red Room were woven in the United States from French Empire designs. The walls are covered by a red twill satin fabric with a gold scroll design in the border. The furniture is upholstered in a silk of the same shade of red. An early 19th-century design inspired the draperies made of gold satin with red silk valances and handmade gold-and-red fringe. The carpet—of beige, red, and gold—is a reproduction of an early 19th-century French Savonnerie carpet in the White House collection; it was made for the room in 1965. The white marble mantel with caryatid figures is one of a pair ordered by Monroe and originally placed in the State Dining Room. The 36-light French Empire chandelier was fashioned from carved and gilded wood about 1805. Carved eagles decorate the sconces on the east wall. Below them is a pair of French lamps of classical design.

This portrait of John James Audubon, exhibited on the west wall, was painted in Edinburgh in 1826 by Scottish artist John Syme. At the time, Audubon was in the British Isles seeking a publisher for his paintings of birds.

Descriptions in contemporary accounts and bills of sale indicate that Monroe purchased furnishings for the Red Room, as well as for the present-day Blue Room, in the prevailing Empire style. This style suited Monroe's desire to furnish the house in a manner that he considered appropriate to the dignity of the nation.

The room was called the Washington Parlor during the Polk and Tyler Administrations, when it contained Gilbert Stuart's portrait of George Washington. President and Mrs. Lincoln used the Red Room frequently for informal entertaining, and a contemporary reporter noted that the furniture was "very rich—of crimson satin and gold damask, with heavy gilded cornices to the windows and a profusion of ormolu work, vases, etc., some of which is very ancient, being bought or presented during Monroe's and Madison's Administrations."

Photographs taken during the latter half of the 19th century indicate that Victorian furnishings had been introduced to the Red Room (see page 130). During the renovation of 1902, many of these furnishings were removed and the collection of First Lady portraits, which had hung there toward the end of the 19th century, was transferred to the Ground Floor Corridor at the request of Edith Kermit Carow Roosevelt.

THE
RED
ROOM

Gilbert Stuart's 1804 portrait of Dolley Madison, hanging on the north wall, is the best-known depiction of the First Lady. When Secretary of State, James Madison commissioned this likeness and one of himself. The paintings hung in the drawing room of their Virginia estate throughout his lifetime.

The American Empire sofa (above) has painted and gilded dolphin feet that curve up to form its scrolled arms. It, and most of the furniture in this room, date to the early 19th century. On the east wall another Empire sofa is flanked by a pair of New York card tables. Above this hang Albert Bierstadt's "Rocky Mountain Landscape," signed and dated 1870; a portrait of Col. William Drayton, painted by Samuel F. B. Morse in 1818; and a pair of English gilded wood sconces with an eagle design. An 1850 still life by Severin Roesen is below Dolley Madison's portrait. The 36-light Empire-style chandelier was made in France of carved and gilded wood.

THE STATE DINING ROOM

The State Dining Room, which now seats as many as 140 guests, was originally much smaller and served at various times as a drawing room, office, and Cabinet Room. Not until the administration of Andrew Jackson was it called the "State Dining Room," although it had been used for formal dinners by previous Presidents.

As the nation grew, so did the invitation list to official functions at the White House. In 1856 a reporter remarked that the State Dining Room was "not large enough, being 30 feet by 25 . . . [A]s the Executive entertains Congress, the Supreme Court, diplomats and most of the distinguished people who visit Washington at his table, he requires a commodious and convenient dining-room." Toward the end of the 19th century, large dinners had to be held in the Cross Hall or in the East Room.

Such inconvenient makeshifts became unnecessary after the renovation of 1902 when architects McKim, Mead & White removed the main stairway from the west end of the Cross Hall and enlarged the State Dining Room to its present dimensions. The two Italian marble mantels installed by Monroe were moved to the Red and Green Rooms; a single larger fireplace was constructed in the west wall. The architecture of the room was modeled after that of neoclassical English houses of the late 18th century. Below a new ceiling and a cornice of white plaster, natural oak wall paneling with Corinthian pilasters and a delicately carved frieze were installed. Three console tables with eagle supports, made by the A. H. Davenport Co. of Boston, were placed against the walls, and a silver-plate chandelier and complementing wall sconces were added.

When furnished, the dining room strongly reflected President Theodore Roosevelt's enthusiasm for big-game hunting. A large moose head (see page 142) was hung above the fireplace, and other big-game trophies were placed on the paneled walls. Two ornate 17th-century Flemish tapestries decorated the room, along with draperies of rich green velvet. An architectural historian hailed the new dining room as "a stately hall of the Early English Renaissance"; a critic, in the *Architectural Record* of April 1903, approvingly wrote that a White House "all carried out in strict Colonial would be but a monotonous and insipid mansion." At the end of his administration Roosevelt had the lions' heads carved on the stone mantel replaced with bison's heads.

The 1902 classical woodwork was preserved in the Truman renovation of 1948-52 and was painted for the first time—a soft celadon green. Roosevelt's big-game trophies had long since been removed from the dining room. (The heads were sent to the Smithsonian Institution in 1923. Mrs. Theodore Roosevelt retrieved five of them in 1934, and six

The mahogany dining table, surrounded by Queen Anne-style chairs, displays part of Monroe's gilt service purchased from France in 1817. The ornamental bronze-doré pieces are used today as table decorations for state dinners. The plateau centerpiece, with seven mirrored sections, measures 13 feet 6 inches in length when fully extended. Standing bacchantes holding wreaths for tiny bowls or candles border the plateau. Three fruit baskets, supported by female figures, may be used to hold flowers. The two rococo-revival candelabra date from the Hayes Administration. The carpet, of soft green and brown, reproduces a Persian design from the 17th century.

THE STATE DINING ROOM

The State Dining Room, sparkling in gold and green, welcomes guests to a state dinner. Vermeil flower bowls and flatware complement the wildflower design of the Lyndon B. Johnson china. Above the mantel hangs George P. A. Healy's contemplative portrait of Abraham Lincoln (right), painted in 1869. The widow of Robert Todd Lincoln, the President's son, bequeathed the portrait to the White House in 1939.

are still there.) During the Truman renovation the original marble mantel with bison's heads was replaced by a simple, black marble mantel; but in 1962, this, in turn, was replaced by a reproduction of the mantel with bison's heads. At that time the wood paneling was painted an antique ivory, and the sconces and chandelier were gilded.

In 1981 the Queen Anne-style chairs, chosen for the room in 1902, were reupholstered in a gold horsehair material, a durable fabric popular in the 19th century. Silk-damask draperies of a golden hue and delicately curved valances were placed over the windows the same year. In 1985, a warm umber glaze was applied to the walls.

Carved into the mantel below George P. A. Healy's portrait of President Lincoln is an inscription from a letter written by John Adams on his second night in the White House: "I Pray Heaven to Bestow the Best of Blessings on THIS HOUSE and on All that shall hereafter Inhabit it. May none but Honest and Wise Men ever rule under this Roof."

THE
FAMILY
DINING
ROOM

The room at the northwest corner of the State Floor, now known as the Family Dining Room, served as the "Public Dining Room" in the early 1800's. It was one of two dining rooms separated by a staircase in James Hoban's original plan (see page 110). President James Monroe held state dinners here, while the other room served as his Cabinet Room.

In the late afternoon, Monroe and his guests gathered in the oval salon—now the Blue Room—before proceeding to the dining room, where the newly purchased French gilt service and vermeil flatware provided an elegant table setting. The guests were seated according to a carefully arranged plan, and Monroe's personal household servants passed the dishes in the formal French manner. When the ladies withdrew after dessert, the gentlemen lingered for a few glasses of wine—Monroe liked to replace the traditional Madeira with a native wine made from scuppernong grapes. Although Americans found the new vermeil service sumptuous, many European dignitaries, expecting more from a chief of state, thought it merely well suited to a private citizen of some means.

The furnishings in the dining room in President Monroe's time were collected by William Lee, a Treasury official and friend of Monroe's, who was his purchasing agent for the refurnishing of the White House following its rebuilding after the fire of 1814. The furniture included two pier tables used by the Madisons in their temporary residences while the White House was being rebuilt and two sideboards, which the Monroes sold to the White House from their personal furnishings. A local craftsman, William Worthington, made a large sideboard for the room, plus a dining table and 16 new chairs. The chairs were all upholstered in glossy black horsehair. Light was provided by four lion's-head sconces, a gilded lamp decorated with swans, and a pair of antique green bronze lamps with stars and swans.

There is little information about the color scheme in the dining room during Monroe's Presidency or, in fact, for much of the 19th century until the Victorian period. The rich Victorian splendor was recorded in contemporary photographs and was finally supplanted in 1902 by a classical-revival style.

Part of President Monroe's 1817 purchases for the White House consisted of a large order from the French silversmith Jacques-Henri Fauconnier (1776-1839). This order included two silver tureens with platters and liners, ladles, a large number of fluted silver plates, serving pieces, and 36 place settings of vermeil flatware. Some of the surviving original pieces, as well as reproduction flatware, are used for state dinners and other entertaining.

The mirrored plateau centerpiece on the table in the Family Dining Room is called "Hiawatha's Boat." Inspired by a poem by Henry Wadsworth Longfellow, its design motifs include a canoe with its sail set and a figure of Hiawatha in its stern. Mrs. Ulysses S. Grant chose the plateau for the White House. A portrait of Brig. Gen. John Hartwell Cocke, mounted on his horse Roebuck, hangs above the fireplace.

A Hepplewhite linen press (above left) is now used for storing silver trays; the coffee urn and tray displayed on the chest are part of the everyday White House silver. A Philadelphia library bookcase of 1800 (center) displays porcelain from the Benjamin Harrison Administration. An original brass pull (top right) from a Sheraton sideboard commemorates George Washington, whose profile is shown in relief. Pieces from early 19th-century flatware services include a vermeil-handled fruit knife, three serving spoons, and a pearl-handled fruit knife.

Eventually, public functions were held in the present State Dining Room, and the Family Dining Room was kept for the private use of the President's family. By the Jackson Administration the size of this room had been reduced by the creation of a butler's pantry at the west end, eliminating an original fireplace and two windows. The architectural details of the room today date from the 1902 renovation, when the vaulted ceiling and cornice with its classical frieze were installed. In 1961, another dining room on the second floor was provided for the family of the President. The Family Dining Room is currently used for official occasions involving a small number of guests.

The painted yellow walls are accented by white woodwork and a white ceiling. Above the cornice is a plaster decoration featuring an eagle. The Louis XVI mantel, acquired in 1962, was made in France in the 1770's. A white eagle appears in decorative relief against its dark green marble. The gilded clock on the mantel is typical of French clocks made for the American trade during the first quarter of the 19th century. Made by Dubuc of Paris, it is decorated with an American eagle and a standing figure of George Washington.

Above the mantel hangs a portrait of Brig. Gen. John Hartwell Cocke of Bremo, Virginia. It was painted in 1859 by Edward Troye, an American artist noted for his paintings of racehorses. General Cocke, in military uniform, is shown at the time of the War of 1812, mounted on his horse Roebuck.

The furniture in the room is from the Federal period. The Sheraton-style mahogany dining table, with finely reeded saber legs, was made in Maryland about 1800. The silver-mirrored centerpiece was made in 1872 by the Gorham Manufacturing Company of Rhode Island and selected for the White House by Mrs. Ulysses S. Grant.

The most important piece of furniture in the room is an early Federal library bookcase, one of a pair built in Philadelphia about 1800. It is made of mahogany with inlaid satinwood bands and quarter fans. This bookcase and its mate in the Mabel Brady Garvan Collection at the Yale University Art Gallery are the only pair of Federal-period American bookcases known to exist.

A New England Federal sideboard of the early 1800's stands along the west wall and has a drapery-effect carving on the sliding tambour door. A Hepplewhite-style mahogany linen press has been modified to provide storage space for silver trays. The linen press, with delicate inlay work, was made in Annapolis about 1790 and once belonged to the family of William Paca, a signer of the Declaration of Independence and later a governor of Maryland.

On the west wall hangs a 1902 portrait of Edith Roosevelt by Theobald Chartran, one of the most sought-after portraitists of the time. Mrs. Roosevelt posed in the colonial garden for the painter, who took some artistic liberties by repositioning the South Portico for his background. Other pictures in the room include several 19th-century American landscapes and a still life by Severin Roesen.

THE
EAST
SITTING
HALL

"All sorts of people come upon all sorts of errands," wrote one of Abraham Lincoln's secretaries, describing the crowds of people who filled the second-floor hall while waiting to see the President. " 'Is Old Abe in?' 'If you mean the President of the United States, this is Congress day. Are you a member of the Senate or of the House? The messenger will take in any member's card.' " Until 1902, when the President's offices were moved to the newly constructed West Wing, dignitaries, inventors, and politicians and their constituents waited in this hall for an opportunity to see the Chief Executive.

Hoban's original Palladian-style fan window dominates the sitting room. Many of the architectural details date from 1952, including the acanthus-leaf-and-bracket cornice, the outer window frame with 13 stars, and the inner frame with circular medallions. The lemon yellow draperies of silk-and-cotton taffeta were hung in 1981. Lighting fixtures include an English cut-glass chandelier of the Georgian period and a pair of Chinese vases made into lamps. The Clintons have personalized the room by using their own Aubusson-style carpet.

In front of the fan window stands a mahogany sofa probably made in New England in the period 1800-10. Flanking it are oval-topped New York breakfast tables with drop leaves, perhaps ten years older. The sofa table was also made early in the 19th century, probably in Boston.

The small tambour desk by the north wall is attributed to English-born craftsmen John and Thomas Seymour, a father and son who opened shop in Boston in 1794. On the same wall is a canterbury—a stand with divisions for music, loose papers, or magazines—probably also made by the Seymours. To the right of the window stands a New England Hepplewhite chest of drawers from about 1790, inlaid with fans, urns, and bellflowers. Two mahogany armchairs, made about 1770, stand in the center of the room: One is English, the other from Philadelphia, part of a set probably made by Thomas Affleck.

Above the tambour desk hangs "Florida Sunrise," painted by Martin Johnson Heade (1819-1904) late in his life, after he had taken up residence in St. Augustine, Florida. The first scene of the southern United States acquired for the White House, this landscape shows the American Luminists' combination of precise drawing and the study of light.

The room contains other works by American artists, including a second painting by Heade "Sailing off the Coast," painted in 1869; Thomas Worthington Whittredge's "Thatcher's Island off Rockport, Massachusetts," painted late in his career in a somewhat impressionistic style; Sydney Laurence's "September Evening, Mount McKinley, Alaska"; and two views of the Golden Gate by Theodore Wores.

This small mahogany tambour desk (right), attributed to
John and Thomas Seymour of Boston, dates from about 1800.
A curly-maple veneer band edges the hinged top, which
folds out to form a writing board. This desk, one of only
three the Seymours made in a pediment design, stands in
the East Sitting Hall. Overlooking the Treasury Building,
this sunny space serves as an informal sitting room for the
adjacent Queens' Suite and Lincoln Suite. During most
of the 19th century the east end of the second floor was
devoted to official business; it is now used by personal,
rather than official, guests of the President's family.

THE QUEENS' BEDROOM

The Queens' Suite, consisting of a small sitting room and a bedroom—called the Rose Guest Room until the mid-1960's—has formed part of the White House family quarters since the Roosevelt renovation of 1902. Previously, these rooms were used by the President's staff. The bedroom was occupied by President Lincoln's private secretaries, John Hay and John G. Nicolay. The sitting room served as Hay's office and years later as an emergency telegraph room while President Garfield struggled to recover from an assassin's bullet.

During the 20th century, the Queens' Suite, sharing the East Sitting Hall with the Lincoln Suite, has been used by a number of royal guests, including Queen Wilhelmina and Queen Juliana of the Netherlands; Queen Frederika of Greece; Great Britain's Queen Elizabeth (now the Queen Mother), Queen Elizabeth II, and Princess Anne—who visited the White House with her brother Prince Charles in 1970. Both Winston Churchill and V. M. Molotov, Soviet Minister for Foreign Affairs, occupied the Queens' Suite at different times while conferring with President Franklin D. Roosevelt during World War II.

The Queens' Bedroom, which overlooks Lafayette Park to the north of the White House, is comfortably furnished in the styles of the American Federal period. Between the windows stands a mahogany tambour bookcase-desk, inlaid with satinwood and curly maple. It is the work of Boston cabinetmakers John and Thomas Seymour. Above it hangs a portrait by Matthew Harris Jouett of Lucy Payne Washington Todd, Dolley Madison's sister. Her marriage to Supreme Court Justice Thomas Todd was the first wedding in the White House.

The four-poster bed is thought to have once belonged to Andrew Jackson. On either side of it are inlaid card tables attributed to the Seymours. A carved Federal sofa displays the fine craftsmanship of Samuel McIntire of Salem, Massachusetts, in its gracefully scrolled arms and the floral decorations of the top rail. Complementing the rose-and-white color scheme is a Hereke carpet from the mid-19th century. The cut-glass chandelier was made in England some 50 years earlier.

The carved wooden mantel on the west wall was formerly in Burnside, a Philadelphia house built in 1792. Above the mantel is a late 17th-century trumeau, a mirror and flower painting framed together. This striking piece was presented to the White House in 1951 by Princess Elizabeth on behalf of her father, King George VI. Also in the room are Thomas Sully's portrait of English actress Fanny Kemble, painted in 1834; a portrait of Emily Donelson, Andrew Jackson's niece and hostess, painted by Ralph E. W. Earl in 1830; and Philip de László's 1921 portrait of Florence Kling Harding.

The Queens' Bedroom, named for its many royal guests, is decorated in shades of rose and white. Most of the fabrics in the room are reproductions of period designs. A Boston window seat from the early 18th century stands at the foot of the bed. The wing chairs by the fireplace were made in Massachusetts between 1800 and 1810. A work table with a fabric bag to hold sewing stands by the chair to the right.

Thomas Sully painted this idealized portrait of English actress Fanny Kemble in 1834 while she was on tour in the United States. Soon after her acclaimed Washington performance, the actress was presented to President Andrew Jackson at the White House.

THE
LINCOLN
BEDROOM

Decorated primarily with American Victorian furnishings from 1850-70, the Lincoln Bedroom is used today as a guest room for friends of the President's family. The Victorian period takes its name from Victoria, Queen of England, and lasted from about 1840 until the end of the century. Several distinctive styles flourished during this period, all based on earlier styles and marked by exaggeration of ornamentation and form. The idea of installing bedroom furniture from the Lincoln era in this room—used by Lincoln as an office and Cabinet Room—came from President Truman. The imposing rosewood bed, more than eight feet

long and almost six feet wide, is thought to have been part of a large quantity of furniture purchased by Mrs. Lincoln in 1861. An 1862 newspaper account indicates that the bed stood in a second-floor guest room; although Abraham Lincoln probably never used the bed, several other Presidents have, including Theodore Roosevelt and Woodrow Wilson. Mrs. Roosevelt was fond of the marble-top rosewood table in the middle of the room, which was probably designed to match the bed. The ornate carving on both pieces of furniture, including fanciful birds, grapevines, and flowers, is typical of the Victorian rococo-revival style.

Between 1830 and 1902 the room now known as the Lincoln Bedroom served Presidents as either an office or a Cabinet Room. When all the second-floor offices were moved to the West Wing during the Roosevelt renovation, this area became part of the private family quarters. The Lincoln Suite, which is now used for personal guests of the President's family and adjoins the East Sitting Hall, includes the bedroom and the Lincoln Sitting Room.

Many of the Victorian furnishings in the bedroom were placed there during the Truman Administration when the patterned Brussels carpet and the Lincoln bed were installed. The chandelier, acquired in 1972, resembles one depicted in an engraving of the room during Lincoln's term. The sofa and three matching chairs, given to the White House in 1954, are believed to have been used in the mansion during the Lincoln Administration. The two identical slipper chairs, also dating from the Lincoln period, are upholstered in antique yellow-and-green Morris velvet; one of the chairs was sold after the President's assassination but was returned to the White House as a gift in 1961.

The rocking chair near the window is similar to the one Lincoln sat in at Ford's Theatre the night of his assassination and is of the period. Round tables, their tops inset with dark marble, flank the bed and are from a set of three bought by President Jackson for the East Room; they were made by the Philadelphia cabinetmaker Anthony Quervelle.

The walnut bureau with full-length mirror has been in the White House for more than a century, although its origins are unknown. In a catalogue of White House furnishings, Mrs. Herbert Hoover noted that a previous resident described the piece as the "old bureau where I used to do my pompadour every morning." Its serpentine curved drawers and ornamental carving are typical Victorian forms. A pair of Argand lamps made in Philadelphia about 1825 provides light for the mirror.

Along the west wall are four of Lincoln's Cabinet chairs, believed to have been purchased for the White House during the Polk Administration. To the left of the fireplace is a desk that Lincoln used at the "summer White House," a brick and stucco cottage on the extensive grounds of the Soldiers' Home—a few miles northeast of the Executive Mansion. The desk was transferred to the White House during the Hoover Administration.

Displayed on the desk is one of five holograph copies of the Gettysburg Address, delivered by President Lincoln on November 19, 1863. The speech dedicated the national cemetery at Gettysburg, Pennsylvania, where Gen. Robert E. Lee's army had been defeated the previous July. This copy, on three sheets of paper, was the second version prepared by Lincoln at the request of historian George Bancroft. The first was returned to Lincoln because it was unsuitable for reproduction by lithography. With it came a request for another, written only on one side of each sheet of paper. Lincoln sent both copies to Col. Alexander Bliss, Bancroft's stepson. The Colonel kept the second copy, since called the "Bliss copy." It is now in the White House. This version is the only

A late-Empire marble-and-ormolu clock, 19 inches high, stands on the mantel in the Lincoln Bedroom. The clock was probably purchased during the Jackson Administration.

one of the five that is signed, dated, and titled by Abraham Lincoln.

Lincoln especially liked the portrait of Andrew Jackson that hangs to the left of the bed. The painting is attributed to Miner K. Kellogg. The portrait of Mary Todd Lincoln to the right of the bed was painted from photographs in 1925 by Katherine Helm, daughter of Mrs. Lincoln's half-sister, Emily Todd Helm. Widow of a Confederate general, Emily Helm visited the White House in 1863 with Katherine. The portrait, given to the White House by Mrs. Robert Todd Lincoln, shows a youthful Mary Lincoln in elegant finery.

Used by President Lincoln as his office, this room over-looked the unfinished Washington Monument and the near-by Virginia hills and was one of the few rooms to escape Mrs. Lincoln's extensive redecorating. An observer in 1862 noted that the room "is very neatly papered, but should be better furnished. All the furniture is exceedingly old, and is too rick-etty to venerate." C. K. Stellwagen commented when he made a sketch of the room (see page 128) in 1864 that the wallpaper was "dark green with a gold star," the carpet "dark green with buff figure in diamonds," and the uphol-stery faded.

Lincoln and his son Tad: an oil miniature painted about 1873 by Francis B. Carpenter, a White House guest in 1864.

Throughout the Civil War an inevitable mass of paperwork littered the office. Maps tracing the course of the war covered the walls; on the desk and tables were newspapers, stacks and bundles of papers, mail, and requests from office seek-ers. Two large wicker wastebaskets held the debris.

To the right of the mantel is an engraving of Francis B. Car-penter's 1864 painting "First Reading of the Emancipation Proclamation before Lincoln's Cabinet." The reading took place in this room on July 22, 1862; the picture shows how the room was furnished at that time. The proclamation, intended by Lincoln primarily as a war measure, declared freedom for all slaves in the regions then in rebellion. Lincoln's Secretary of State William Sew-ard advised him that the proclamation should be delayed until after a military victory by Union forces to make it appear an act of national strength—not a despairing last resort.

The Battle of Antietam provided a Union victory, and on September 22 a preliminary proclamation was issued, to become effective when signed by the President in 100 days. In this room, following the tradi-tional New Year's reception of January 1, 1863, President Lincoln signed the proclamation—and gave it the force of law.

An 1865 lithograph entitled "Abraham Lincoln's Last Reception" hangs above the desk. It shows the President and the First Lady receiv-ing guests, including Cabinet members and prominent generals, in the East Room. On the north wall hangs a 1931 portrait of Lincoln by Ste-phen Arnold Douglas Volk, based on a bust his father, Leonard Volk, made from life. Many other objects depicting or associated with Presi-dent Lincoln have been placed in the room.

THE LINCOLN SITTING ROOM

The Lincoln Sitting Room is furnished in late-Empire and Victorian styles to harmonize with the decor of the adjoining Lincoln Bedroom. A small corner room, it served as a busy office for Presidential staff members during most of the 19th century.

The small room at the southeast corner of the second floor was apparently little used in the mansion's early years. As late as 1825, an inventory described it simply as "empty." However, English novelist Charles Dickens, in an account of his visit to the White House during the Tyler Administration, wrote that the room was then used as the President's office, although he was not favorably impressed with either its size or its furnishings. During the Polk Administration, it doubled as a bedroom and office for the President's nephew and private secretary, J. Knox Walker. The room continued to be used as an office for various Presidential clerks and secretaries until 1902, when all offices were moved to the newly constructed West Wing. It then became part of the family quarters.

The present decor of burgundy, gold, and cream, which complements the Victorian character of the adjoining Lincoln Bedroom, dates from the Clinton Administration. Bold patterned paper covering the ceiling, burgundy silk draperies and swags with gilt decorations, and alternating medallions and rosettes in the carpet—woven in 36-inch strips as was popular in America after 1850—continue the color scheme. Painted a gold tone, the window frames, chair rail, and cornice highlight cream-colored walls. The cut-glass chandelier is probably American and dates from about 1860. Diamond-pointed prisms circle its shaft and hang from its six candle arms.

On the north wall stands a mahogany and marble fall-front desk, a reproduction of an Empire piece bought by James Monroe when he was minister to France and reputedly used by him in the White House. The desk is one of seven pieces that Mrs. Herbert Hoover had copied in 1932 for what she called the "Monroe Room"—now the Treaty Room.

The ebonized wood side chair with a rounded shield back, one of a pair in the room, bears a bronze plaque on its crest identifying it as part of a suite given to friends by President and Mrs. Lincoln in 1862. The center table on the west wall, made in America about 1880 in the Louis XVI-revival style, is fashioned from plain and burl walnut with marquetry designs of agricultural implements, flowers, and musical instruments. During the late 19th century, it and the matching sofa and chair now in this room were all Green Room furnishings.

In addition to numerous engravings and mementos of Lincoln's time, the sitting room contains "The Republican Court in the Days of Lincoln," painted by Peter F. Rothermel about 1867 (see pages 122-23); an oil of Ulysses S. Grant painted in 1875 by Henry Ulke; and a butterfly made on folded paper by Albert Bierstadt in 1893—similar to those he made for the Hayes family during a White House stay in 1878.

THE
TREATY
ROOM

The Treaty Room is now President Clinton's office and sitting room in the Residence. This second-floor room has served in many capacities. For some early 19th-century Presidents, it was a private meeting room; during the Lincoln Administration, it was the waiting room for the adjoining President's Office—now the Lincoln Bedroom. President Andrew Johnson began meeting here with his Cabinet in 1866, and it was used as the Cabinet Room until Presidential staff offices were moved to the West Wing in 1902. After Mrs. Herbert Hoover furnished the room as a parlor with objects from the Monroe era and reproductions of furniture that once belonged to President Monroe, it became known as the Monroe Room.

In 1961 the room was furnished to resemble the Cabinet Room during President Ulysses S. Grant's term of office. Victorian furnishings placed here at that time included many pieces bought for the room by Grant in 1869, as well as others of a similar style that had been used elsewhere in the White House since the late 19th century.

The name "Treaty Room" was chosen during the administration of John F. Kennedy to reflect the many important decisions made here. One of the earliest occasions was August 12, 1898, when the peace protocol establishing an armistice in the Spanish-American War was signed by French Ambassador Jules Cambon on behalf of the Spanish government and by William R. Day, the U. S. Secretary of State. President John F. Kennedy signed the U. S. instrument of ratification of the Treaty for a Partial Nuclear Test Ban on October 7, 1963; and on September 30, 1972, President Richard M. Nixon signed the U. S. instrument of ratification of the Treaty on the Limitation of Anti-Ballistic Missile Systems.

In 1993, the room was decorated as an office and sitting room for President Clinton, incorporating 19th-century furnishings from the White House collection. The walls are covered to simulate red leather; red-and-blue draperies are topped with walnut cornices decorated with gilded gesso wreaths; and matching walnut woodwork replaced the painted trim installed in the Truman Administration. A gilded metal chandelier with a spread-eagle finial, used in the Red Room from 1902 to 1948, was placed here, as was a 19th-century Persian Heriz carpet.

The elaborate, gilded overmantel mirror that dominates the east wall is one of a pair bought for the Green Room during the Franklin Pierce Administration. Made of wood and gesso, its crest work features a large U. S. shield. The Italian marble mantel beneath it was purchased in 1902 for this room. An inscription on the mantel's central panel states: "This room was first used for meetings of the Cabinet during the Administration of President Johnson. It continued to be so used until the year

The Treaty Room, a second-floor office and sitting room for the President, now incorporates the conference table that was used when this room was the Cabinet Room in the late 19th century. The ornate gilded overmantel mirror and handsome chandelier were both originally bought for and used on the State Floor. Bookcases were added in 1993 when the easy chair and ottoman belonging to the Clintons were placed here.

MCMII. Here the treaty of peace with Spain was signed." In the fireplace is a pair of brass andirons with Chinese design motifs, made in America about 1840. They are believed to have been used in the Residence during the Zachary Taylor Administration; and they remained in the Taylor family until they were presented to the White House.

When Benjamin Franklin was in London in 1758, he commissioned from Benjamin Wilson the portrait now on the south wall. Taken from Franklin's house during the Revolutionary War, it was given to the United States in 1906 in honor of the bicentenary of Franklin's birth.

The magnificent walnut table, together with a set of "walnut French overstuffed chairs," was ordered in 1869 by President Grant for his Cabinet Room from Pottier & Stymus Manufacturing Co. in New York. During the renovation of 1902 the Cabinet chairs were sold as souvenirs to Theodore Roosevelt's Cabinet members for a token $5 apiece. The table was returned to the Treaty Room in 1993 for use as a desk by President Clinton. This massive Victorian piece is fitted with locking drawers in which President Grant and his seven Cabinet officers could keep their papers. It is uncertain how the eighth Cabinet member was accommodated after the Department of Agriculture was created in 1889, but the table continued in use until 1902.

On March 26, 1979, President Jimmy Carter had the conference table

THE TREATY ROOM

The conference table used as a desk by President Clinton was part of a suite ordered by President Grant from the New York firm of Pottier & Stymus for use in this room. The table is fitted with eight locking drawers—at that time, enough for the President and each member of his Cabinet. The table continued in use here until 1902, when the Cabinet moved to the West Wing. In 1961 Mrs. Kennedy installed the desk and the remaining matching pieces in this room, renamed the Treaty Room.

placed on the north grounds for the signing of the peace treaty between Egypt and Israel that followed the Camp David agreements. For the signing of the Israeli-Palestinian accord on September 13, 1993, and the declaration ending the state of war between Jordan and Israel on July 25, 1994, President Clinton had it placed on the South Lawn.

The table and original chairs appear in an 1899 painting on the west wall—Theobald Chartran's "The Signing of the Peace Protocol Between Spain and the United States, August 12, 1898." Also displayed in this room is the three-handled silver cup, made by Louis C. Tiffany, that was presented to French Ambassador Jules Cambon on this historic occasion by President William McKinley.

On the north wall hangs "The Peacemakers," painted by George P. A. Healy in 1868. It depicts a meeting aboard the *River Queen* in 1865, during the siege of Richmond, Virginia. The steamer had brought President Lincoln to General Ulysses S. Grant's headquarters on the James River to discuss prospects for ending the war. Healy's portrait of Lincoln in the State Dining Room was based on the likeness in this picture. Beneath the painting is a circular mahogany-and-marble table that bears the label of Anthony Quervelle of Philadelphia. It and two smaller tables were bought by President Andrew Jackson in 1829 for placement under the three chandeliers in the newly completed East Room.

THE CENTER HALL

The Center Hall, brightened by a yellow-and-white color scheme, serves as a spacious drawing room for the First Family and Presidential guests, including many foreign dignitaries, who are received in the Yellow Oval Room. When the eastern end of the second floor was used for Presidential offices, the Center Hall area, then known as the "Great Passage," contained a partition to keep the public from wandering into the private quarters. President Arthur made the western end of the hall into a "picture gallery, promenade, and smoking room."

During World War II, as playwright Robert Sherwood recalled, the long corridor was dark and dismal, cluttered by ships' models, prints, old photographs, and hundreds of books. The area was redesigned as a sitting room during the Truman renovation of 1948-52. It was unified by the installation of a cornice, bookshelves, and a pair of late 18th-century English chandeliers.

Recent First Families have used the Center Hall to display paintings by American artists. Toward its west end hangs Mary Cassatt's "Young Mother and Two Children," which reveals the influence of French artists Manet and Degas. Three other important American paintings are placed in the area. "Spring in the Valley" was painted by Willard Leroy Metcalf, a committed Impressionist. The artist painted this vital New England scene around 1924, near the end of his life. Thomas Eakins's 1903 painting "Ruth" displays the traits that earned the artist a reputation for portraits of unyielding realism and insightful characterization. The bold abstract "Untitled XXXIX" by Dutch-born Willem de Kooning is on loan from the artist's collection. Also displayed here is "Still Life with Quince, Apples, and Pears," a vibrantly colored example of French Impressionist Paul Cézanne's work, as well as a 1992 Arkansas landscape from the Clintons' private collection.

The octagonal pedestal writing desk, which divides the hall into two spaces, was donated to the White House during the Kennedy Administration. This English partners' desk dates from the late 18th century and is made in two halves that may be separated for use against a wall or combined in the center of a room.

Other pieces made in the late 18th or early 19th centuries include the New England sofa table in front of the shelves on the north wall, the pair of mahogany Chippendale looking glasses on either side of the entrance to the West Sitting Hall, and the two matching English Regency-style stands of gilded and painted wood that flank the door to the Yellow Oval Room. The fine Sheraton-style chairback settee and four matching chairs were made in Philadelphia. A palace scene decorates the antique 12-panel Chinese coromandel screen along the south wall.

Filled with furnishings from the 18th and 19th centuries, the Center Hall serves as an informal sitting room for the President's family and guests and as a reception area for the Yellow Oval Room, to the left.

The mahogany chairback settee (below) and four matching chairs in
the Center Hall are among the finest existing examples of Philadelphia
craftsmanship in the Sheraton style. They date from the years 1800-10.

Willard Leroy Metcalf painted the peaceful landscape "Spring in the Valley" (above) about 1924. Early in his career the artist specialized in figure painting and illustration; this landscape is in the impressionist style he used in his later years. The mahogany card table (left), with a folding top, is one of a pair bearing fine satinwood inlay. These Federal-period tables are attributed to cabinetmakers John and Thomas Seymour of Boston.

THE
CENTER
HALL

As an adult, the subject of "Ruth," a 1903 painting (right) by Thomas Eakins, talked about how she hated to dress up and pose for the artist. That mood shows clearly in this portrait. Appreciated today for his realism and insight, Eakins's severe, carefully executed paintings earned him little recognition during his lifetime. "Young Mother and Two Children" (below) was painted by Mary Cassatt in 1908. Born in Pennsylvania, the artist spent most of her life in France. Children were a favorite subject, and she painted them with strength and without sentimentality. Her work, noted for its color and directness, is associated with the Impressionists.

THE YELLOW OVAL ROOM

On New Year's Day, 1801, President John Adams held the first White House reception in this oval room which, although incomplete, contained some handsome furnishings and was greatly admired. During Thomas Jefferson's term, this room was called the "Ladies' Drawing Room," and the President's married daughters, when visiting their father, entertained friends here. In 1809, Dolley Madison had the furniture upholstered in yellow damask and had curtains—with festoons and fringes—made of the same material. All the original furnishings were destroyed in the fire of 1814. After numerous changes in use and appearance, the oval drawing room was furnished in the Louis XVI style during the Kennedy Administration. The yellow color scheme chosen again at that time continues as the dominant theme; but the formality has been softened by the addition of two overstuffed sofas.

Architectural changes made in the room in 1974 included adding a chair rail and a plaster ceiling centerpiece. This oval ceiling medallion echoes the shape of the room; it bears the acanthus-leaf and swag motifs that were prominent in Louis XVI neoclassical designs. The furniture, too, reflects the period. It is distinguished by tapered, sometimes fluted, chair legs; delicately carved chair and sofa frames painted in pale colors; and square or oval chairbacks.

The rare set of four carved and gilded armchairs was made by Jean-Baptiste-Claude Sené, a well-known French craftsman of the Louis XVI period. Between two of the chairs stands a small writing table of the same period, which bears the stamp of Jean-François Leleu, another famous French cabinetmaker. Its top drawer contains a compartment with inkwell and sand holder. A painted settee and two armchairs, part of an American suite of a slightly later period, once belonged to President Monroe. They are decorated with scrollwork and female figures. The suite of Louis XVI furniture, made about 1800 by Jean-Baptiste Lelarge, includes two side chairs and four armchairs.

Female figures, carved in high relief, decorate the early 19th-century Italian marble mantel. Pistol-handled Chinese urns on the mantel date to the same period, and the gilt-bronze clock between them shows French workmanship of the 18th century.

Two elaborately inlaid French commodes of the Louis XV style flank the mantel. The pair of candelabra that now stands on the commodes was a gift from the British government, presented by Princess Elizabeth during her 1951 visit to the United States. Intricately crafted from marble, bronze-doré, and blue spar stone, they were made in England

The Yellow Oval Room, decorated in the Louis XVI style of late 18th-century France, serves as a formal drawing room for the President's family and as a reception room for foreign chiefs of state and heads of government before state luncheons and dinners. The colors of its furnishings reflect the name of the room: yellow silk draperies, installed in 1972; an antique Turkish Hereke rug, added in 1974; and two comfortable sofas, upholstered in yellow damask and placed here in 1981. Paintings by late 19th-century American artists displayed in the room include Jasper Cropsey's "Under the Palisades in October," which hangs above the mantel.

Displayed in the President's Dining Room is a coffee set with ivory handles made in Paris around 1809-19 by Martin-Guillaume Biennais. It was part of a silver table service purchased for the White House in 1833.

Taylor's occupancy that was described in a contemporary account as "made filthy by tobacco-chewers." She had a used Brussels carpet cleaned, sent for her piano and her daughter's harp, and made this room the library when Congress appropriated $2,000 to purchase books for the White House; it remained a library through the 1920's. During the Hayes Administration the library also contained an upright piano. An 1880 newspaper engraving shows Secretary of Interior Carl Schurz playing it for the entertainment of the assembled Hayes family. In 1889, according to an aide to President Benjamin Harrison, the first White House Christmas tree was displayed here.

Grover Cleveland, as well as Benjamin Harrison, used this room as an office. After Harrison it became a sitting room until Franklin D. Roosevelt made it his study. Here, on December 7, 1941, he first learned that the Japanese had bombed Pearl Harbor. In the "oval study" both he and President Harry S. Truman used a desk that Queen Victoria presented to the White House during the Hayes Administration. The desk was made of timbers from H.M.S. *Resolute*, a British ship saved by American whalers in the Arctic after it was abandoned during a rescue mission in 1854, refitted, and returned to the Queen from the United States. President Clinton now uses it in the Oval Office.

Today, the Yellow Oval Room serves as a formal drawing room for the President and his family and as a reception room for foreign visitors attending state dinners and luncheons. The room gives access to the Truman Balcony. Overlooking the South Lawn, the balcony offers a panorama of the Ellipse, the Washington Monument, and the Jefferson Memorial. Many First Families have used the balcony for dining, entertaining guests, and viewing Fourth of July fireworks.

"Cliffs of Green River, Wyoming," completed in 1910 by American artist Thomas Moran, hangs to the left of the mantel. Moran's use of lush colors and his stylistic treatment of light and atmosphere reflect the influence of his teacher, English romantic painter J.M.W. Turner. Moran accompanied several geological expeditions to unexplored regions of the West, and his landscapes provided dramatic records of these wild areas.

87

Displayed in the President's Dining Room is a coffee set with ivory handles made in Paris around 1809-19 by Martin-Guillaume Biennais. It was part of a silver table service purchased for the White House in 1833.

The Yellow Oval Room, decorated in the Louis XVI style of late 18th-century France, serves as a formal drawing room for the President's family and as a reception room for foreign chiefs of state and heads of government before state luncheons and dinners. The colors of its furnishings reflect the name of the room: yellow silk draperies, installed in 1972; an antique Turkish Hereke rug, added in 1974; and two comfortable sofas, upholstered in yellow damask and placed here in 1981. Paintings by late 19th-century American artists displayed in the room include Jasper Cropsey's "Under the Palisades in October," which hangs above the mantel.

about 1770. The Empire-style chandelier of bronze-doré and crystal was made in France about 1820. The two large vertical mirrors on the west wall, with Adam-style carved and gilded frames, are English, dating from the late 18th century. Under the mirrors stand two carved and gilded console tables. Half-moon in shape, they feature elaborate openwork carving along the apron. Formerly in the collection of the Chateau de Condé, they were acquired by the White House in 1973. The carpet is a 19th-century Turkish Hereke, woven in a French design.

Noteworthy paintings by American artists hang in the Yellow Oval Room. To the left of the door leading from the Center Hall is "Shinnicock Hills, Long Island," an impressionist landscape painted by William Merritt Chase in 1900. Albert Bierstadt's study of storm clouds, from about 1880, hangs to the right of this door. On the west wall hangs the 1877 painting "Castle Rock, Nahant, Massachusetts," by Alfred T. Bricher, who was known for his scenes of the Massachusetts coast. A cityscape, "New York Harbor and the Battery," painted by Andrew Melrose about 1887, is displayed on the east wall, along with "Cliffs of Green River, Wyoming," a majestic and romantic view of the American West by Thomas Moran, and "Mouth of the Delaware," a scene of sailing vessels and smaller fishing boats painted by Thomas Birch in 1928. Jasper Cropsey's "Under the Palisades in October" hangs over the fireplace. This 1895 painting of cliffs along the Hudson River illustrates the reverence for wilderness that characterizes the Hudson River School, the first truly American school of artists.

According to an inventory of 1825, the Yellow Oval Room was used as a bedroom; it became a family room during the administration of Andrew Jackson. Mrs. Fillmore found a straw carpet left from President

"New York Harbor and the Battery," by New Jersey landscape artist Andrew Melrose, provides a glimpse of the waterfront in lower Manhattan about 1887. The Statue of Liberty, which was unveiled on October 28, 1886, appears in the background.

THE YELLOW OVAL ROOM

THE PRESIDENT'S DINING ROOM

Until it was converted into a dining room in 1961, this large northwest room on the second floor had been used as a family bedroom or sitting room. In the 19th century, it served as a bedroom for children of Presidents, including Tad Lincoln, and for relatives, such as Mr. and Mrs. Andrew Jackson Donelson. President and Mrs. Grover Cleveland and also President and Mrs. William McKinley used the room as their bedroom. When visiting the White House much later, Alice Roosevelt Longworth recalled that in this room her appendix had been removed.

Now furnished in American Federal styles, many of its pieces, including the Sheraton pedestal dining table made between 1800 and 1815, were given to the White House in 1961 and 1962. The side chairs, whose shield backs have splats with Prince of Wales plumes, date to 1790-1800. Wilson china, Kennedy glassware, and flatware first ordered during the Coolidge Administration comprise the place settings. The English chandelier above the table is from the 18th century; the silk-and-wool Turkish Hereke carpet is from the 19th century.

Between the windows a rosewood pier table ornamented with gilt mounts holds a pair of English candelabra with Wedgwood panels. Daniel Webster is thought to have owned the American sideboard on the west wall. Its document drawers are inlaid with the initials "D. W." A gilded girandole mirror hangs above the sideboard.

A bookcase on the east wall displays silver bought by Andrew Jackson for the White House in 1833 from the estate of the Russian Minister Baron de Tuyll. Some of the pieces carry the mark of noted French silversmith Martin-Guillaume Biennais. Jackson was sharply criticized at the time for spending more than $4,000 in federal funds for the silver, although it is now recognized that the money was well spent.

The wooden mantel on the east wall was made in Philadelphia about 1815. Its decorations, attributed to Robert Wellford, include the famous words spoken by Commodore Oliver Hazard Perry after the Battle of Lake Erie during the War of 1812: "We have met the enemy, and they are ours." The small mahogany sideboard to the right of the entrance to the hall is attributed to Annapolis cabinetmaker John Shaw.

The wallpaper in this room, called "The War of Independence," is a later version of the 1834 Zuber paper in the Diplomatic Reception Room. American landscapes, based on engravings made in the 1820's by Engelmann, form the background for the somewhat fanciful scenes of the Revolution. To the left of the windows, General Washington triumphantly enters Boston in 1776. (The State House, which appears on the city skyline, was not in fact completed until 1798.) Between the windows is an imaginary battle near Virginia's Natural Bridge.

The President's Dining Room, which serves as a convenient place for family meals and private entertainment, is furnished in styles of the American Federal period. A Hereke carpet and draperies of blue and green silk damask were chosen to complement the historical wallpaper.

THE WEST SITTING HALL

Family photographs massed on tables flanking the sofa personalize the West Sitting Hall. Decorated with comfortable contemporary furniture and American antiques and reproductions, the hall serves as a private living room for the Clinton family. In the afternoon, sun pouring through the fan window adds a warm glow to the yellow-and-white color scheme.

The West Sitting Hall, overlooking the West Wing and the Old Executive Office Building, was little more than a glorified stair landing until the renovation of 1902. During the 19th century this area was as sparsely furnished as the Center Hall. Occasionally a detail caught the attention of a visitor or reporter—a special correspondent in the Hayes Administration singled out the "RICH BUT FRIGHTFULLY UGLY CARPET."

After 1902 the hall became a private sitting area; successive Presidential families furnished it with favorite items of their own to re-create the atmosphere of home. Eleanor Roosevelt closed off the west hall with screens and ordered bright chintz slipcovers for the sofas and chairs; her social secretary considered it "really the most cheery and comfortable spot in the White House." This was where the family gathered for afternoon tea and where Mrs. Roosevelt presided over the traditional morning coffee with family, staff members, and guests. During the Truman renovation of 1948-52, the architects turned the hall into a room by enclosing it with solid partitions and pocket doors.

"Morning on the Seine, Good Weather" (left), by Claude Monet, hangs on the north wall of the West Sitting Hall. One of a series of 18 similar views painted in 1897 to record the changing effects of light and color, it was given to the White House in 1963 by the Kennedy family in memory of President John F. Kennedy.

THE
WEST
WING

Well before the end of the 19th century, it had become clear that the cramped quarters of the second floor of the White House were no longer adequate for the offices of the President and his staff. An additional disadvantage was the lack of privacy for the Presidential family.

To solve the problem, Congress appropriated $65,196 for the construction of the West Wing in 1902. The architectural firm of McKim, Mead & White, under considerable pressure from President Theodore Roosevelt to complete the addition rapidly, proposed a modest temporary structure; the problem of building "a permanent, adequate, and thoroughly dignified office" was to be settled later.

In fact, the West Wing has remained at its original site although it was doubled in size in 1909 and further enlarged in 1934. Additional offices for executive personnel are located to the west of the White House in the ornate Old Executive Office Building, begun during Grant's term of office to house the State, War, and Navy Departments. The remodeling of the West Wing in 1969 added a new driveway and portico on the north side, which provided a more formal entrance and reception area for the President's callers.

The foyer leading to the West Wing Reception Room contains a statue of Nathan Hale modeled by Frederick William MacMonnies in 1890. This small bronze version of a life-size figure standing in New York's City Hall Park was cast in Paris by H. Rouard.

THE WEST WING RECEPTION ROOM: Also called the Appointments Lobby, this room was created in 1969 from the former Press Lobby. Between two sofas copied from an original piece in the Governor's Palace in Williamsburg stands a late 18th-century English library bookcase.

Large paintings hang on either side of the bookcase. English artist William John Huggins's "The First Naval Action in the War of 1812" was painted in 1816. It shows the naval division of Commodore John Rodgers pursuing the British frigate H.M.S. *Belvidera* five days after the United States declared war on Great Britain. The painting was probably based on a sketch made by an officer aboard the British ship. To the right hangs "Lake Among the Hills," an 1858 depiction of Lake Mohonk in New York State, by Scottish-born artist William M. Hart. Brought to the United States as a child, Hart worked as an itinerant portrait painter, returned to Scotland to study art, then set himself up in New York City as a landscape specialist.

A. Wordsworth Thompson's "Cannonading on the Potomac, October, 1861," on the north wall, was based on sketches he made during the Battle of Ball's Bluff, near Leesburg, Virginia, on October 21, 1861. To its right hangs a scene of surf crashing on a rocky shore, "Rough Sea

Works of 19th- and 20th-century artists are displayed in the West Wing Reception Room. "The First Naval Action in the War of 1812," by William John Huggins, hangs to the left of the library bookcase; to the right is William M. Hart's 1858 landscape "Lake Among the Hills." The gilded wood gallery clock was made in Massachusetts about 1810.

"Rutland Falls, Vermont," painted in 1848 by Frederic E. Church, emphasizes the effect of light and clouds.

at Bailey's Island, Maine," painted in 1909 by Frederick Judd Waugh.

The gilded gallery clock on the west wall was made about 1810 by Simon Willard, most prominent member of a well-known family of clocksmiths of Roxbury, Massachusetts. To its right is "Rutland Falls, Vermont" by Frederic E. Church. Painted in 1848, the somewhat idealized landscape shows the artist's careful depiction of nature and use of light and clouds for dramatic effect.

Portraits of two Presidents hang in the room. An inscription on the back of the 1841 likeness of John Tyler indicates that James Reid Lambdin painted the head, from life, in Washington and finished the small full-length portrait in Philadelphia. Eliphalet Frazer Andrews painted this copy of John Vanderlyn's portrait of Zachary Taylor in 1879.

The West Wing Reception Room today bears little resemblance to the Press Lobby that was located here from the early 1900's to the late 1960's. During those years, the room was usually filled with reporters and photographers sitting and reading in large, worn leather armchairs and sofas—or racing to their telephones when a White House news story broke. Current arrangements give the news media space where an indoor swimming pool used to be, in the area connecting the West Wing and the Residence.

THE ROOSEVELT ROOM: Staff meetings and occasional press conferences take place in the Roosevelt Room. Its former name, the Fish Room, was acquired during the time of Franklin D. Roosevelt, when it contained an aquarium and mementos of the President's fishing trips. Roosevelt's staff, however, nicknamed the room "the morgue" because so many callers sat "cooling off" in it. President Kennedy continued the Fish Room decor, displaying a mounted sailfish on one wall.

The Roosevelt Room, furnished with Queen Anne and Chippendale reproductions, provides a convenient place for meetings of all kinds. An early 20th-century bookcase standing against the west wall contains bound volumes of Presidential papers.

The carved wooden mantel on the east wall was made for the White House in 1902 and was installed in this room in 1934. Above the mantel is Tade Styka's dramatic equestrian portrait of Theodore Roosevelt, painted about 1909. Two metal plaques with profile portraits are displayed on the wall: James Earle Fraser's Theodore Roosevelt, cast about 1920, and John DeStefano's Franklin D. Roosevelt, sculpted in 1933.

Alfred Jonniaux's portrait of Franklin Roosevelt, painted from photographs in 1958, hangs on the south wall. Beside it is "View of the City of Washington from the Virginia Shore," painted by William MacLeod in 1856 from a spot near Alexandria. "Our Vanishing Wildlife," the bronze below it, was sculpted by Alexander Pope about 1915 and shows a bison battling three wolves. The mahogany tall case clock was made in Wilmington, Delaware, about 1830 and has works by Charles Canby. The room also contains the gold medallion presented to Theodore Roosevelt in 1906 when he received a Nobel prize for mediating the peace settlement after the Russo-Japanese War.

The Roosevelt Room, a staff meeting room, was named by President Nixon to honor both Theodore and Franklin Roosevelt for their parts in making the West Wing a reality. Tade Styka painted the equestrian portrait of Theodore Roosevelt (right) about 1909.

THE WEST WING

THE CABINET ROOM: *Since 1902 the Cabinet has met in the West Wing. This room, which looks out on the Rose Garden, has been used since 1934. Cabinet meetings regularly include the Department Secretaries and other officials appointed by the President. The room is also used for National Security Council sessions, meetings with Congressional leaders and Presidential advisers, and for special award presentations.*

The chairs, copies of a late 18th-century American style, bear brass plaques with Cabinet members' titles. Marble busts of George Washington and Benjamin Franklin rest in niches flanking the fireplace. Edouard-Armand Dumaresque's "The Signing of the Declaration of Independence" was chosen to hang over the mantel. The room also displays portraits of Presidents Washington, Jefferson, Lincoln, and Theodore Roosevelt.

THE
WEST
WING

Antique furniture and works of art adorn the President's Oval Office. Its decor may vary from one administration to another, but the flags standing behind the desk remain in their traditional places: to the President's left, the Presidential flag; to his right, in the place of honor, the flag of the United States of America.

THE PRESIDENT'S OVAL OFFICE: The Chief Executive meets formally with visiting chiefs of state and heads of government in the Oval Office. Built in 1909, it was moved in 1934 from the center of the West Wing to its southeast corner. The room's architectural features include pediments over the doors, shell canopies above the windows and the west wall niches, and the Presidential seal in low relief set into the ceiling.

The Oval Office reflects each change of administration dramatically. Most Presidents fill it with personal mementos, such as the photographs of family members and friends that President Clinton displays on the table behind his desk. The desk chosen by President Clinton was given to Rutherford B. Hayes by Queen Victoria in 1880 and is made of oak timbers from H.M.S. *Resolute*, a ship recovered by American whalers in the Arctic. Franklin D. Roosevelt ordered the panel bearing the Presidential coat of arms for its kneehole. The coat of arms also appears in the specially woven oval carpet. It and gold damask draperies with fabric of an 18th-century pattern were placed in the room in 1993.

Matching antique Chinese vases adorn a marble mantel with classical lines, which has been in the Oval Office since 1909. Above the mantel hangs a "porthole" portrait of George Washington by Rembrandt Peale, showing Washington in Continental Army uniform.

Scenes of 19th-century America flank the mantel. Thomas Moran's "The Three Tetons," painted about 1895, appears here; on the other side is George Cooke's 1833 painting "City of Washington From Beyond the Navy Yard." A bronze bust of Benjamin Franklin by noted French sculptor Jean-Antoine Houdon rests beneath the Moran.

The mahogany case of the clock standing against the east wall was made in the early 19th century by prominent Boston cabinetmakers John and Thomas Seymour. Beside it is Frederic Remington's bronze "The Bronco Buster." On the south wall hangs "The Avenue in the Rain" by Childe Hassam (see page 4).

THE
WEST
WING

THE ROSE GARDEN: At the west end of the Rose Garden, French doors open from the Cabinet Room onto a white-pillared colonnade similar in style to the adjoining west terrace pavilion, which connects the West Wing to the Executive Residence. Much as the Jacqueline Kennedy Garden on the east side of the mansion is frequently used by the First Lady to receive her guests, the Rose Garden often serves as a reception area for the President.

Visitors traditionally welcomed here include foreign dignitaries and Medal of Honor recipients. The first team of United States astronauts and the first woman to be appointed to the Supreme Court of the U. S. were also received in the Rose Garden. It is used for occasional press conferences and has served as the setting for elegant state dinners, as in 1976 during the Bicentennial visit of Queen Elizabeth II of Great Britain. The Rose Garden was the scene of the first outdoor White House wedding when Tricia Nixon married Edward Cox in June 1971. In June of 1994, when Emperor Akihito of Japan was visiting, President and Mrs. Clinton chose the Rose Garden as the setting for their first state dinner: 182 guests dined under a tent decorated with thousands of roses.

Roses were first planted here by Ellen Axson Wilson in 1913. Except for minor alterations in 1934 and during the 1948-52 renovation, no changes were made in the garden until 1962 when, at the request of President Kennedy, Mrs. Paul Mellon redesigned it.

As early as 1800, the first White House garden was being planned for President John Adams. A Washingtonian recorded in a diary on March 20 of that year: "After breakfast we walked . . . to the ground behind the President's House, which [will be] enclosed and laid out for a garden. It is at present in great confusion, having on it old brick kilns, pits to contain Water used by the brick makers. . . ." The writer failed to mention the type of garden planned for this area.

By 1902, forcing beds, greenhouses, and conservatories occupied the site selected for the new West Wing. Demolition of the "glass houses" uncovered a large part of Thomas Jefferson's west pavilion, which was restored to lead to the new executive offices. This restoration and the rebuilding of the east pavilion clearly show the efforts of Theodore Roosevelt and the architects of the West Wing to maintain the original character and plan of the historic mansion.

The Rose Garden follows the plan of a traditional 18th-century American garden. Framed by osmanthus and boxwood, planting beds—with flowering crab apples set in them—form the long lines of the rectangle. Flowers provide color to the beds from early spring until frost comes.

*F6

F7

*F9

*F8

*F5

*F3

*F2

F4

G6

G5

*G2

G4

G3

A cutaway view of the White House—
with the South Portico in the foreground—
reveals the mansion's interior. Visitors
who take the public guided tour walk along
the glass-enclosed colonnade to the Ground
Floor Corridor, climb the stairs to the
State Floor, visit four state reception
rooms and the State Dining Room, then
depart by way of the North Entrance.

Ground Floor
G1 Library
*G2 Ground Floor Corridor
G3 Vermeil Room
G4 China Room
G5 Diplomatic Reception Room
G6 Map Room

State Floor
*F1 East Room
*F2 Green Room
*F3 Blue Room
F4 South Portico
*F5 Red Room
*F6 State Dining Room
F7 Family Dining Room
*F8 Cross Hall
*F9 Entrance Hall

*An asterisk marks rooms
open to the public.

ROBERT W. NICHOLSON

THE CHANGING
WHITE HOUSE

BY MARY ANN HARRELL

"Long live George Washington, President of the United States!" A cheering crowd in front of Federal Hall in New York City hailed the man who had just taken an oath of office—blending the ancient salutation to a king and the new title for a new kind of executive.

Thus for decades old forms and new experiments would shape the life of a nation. In 1789 the United States of America began working out a second try at self-government under the new Constitution; and this, for a free people, meant a variety of undertakings: from passing new laws to paving the streets of a capital city, and agreeing on republican manners for a President's dinner party.

By July 12, 1790, President Washington was signing an Act of Congress to fix Philadelphia as temporary capital until the "first Monday in December, 1800," when the federal government would take up residence in a district "not exceeding ten miles square . . . on the river Potomac." After long wrangling over a location, Secretary of State Thomas Jefferson and Secretary of the Treasury Alexander Hamilton had bargained their way to a supper-table agreement that Congress would approve.

Ten years may have seemed more than adequate for preparing the Capital. It wasn't. Not until mid-March 1792 did the three Commissioners of the Federal City set up competitions for the design of a building for the Congress and a house for the President, with Jefferson writing an announcement for the newspapers.

George Washington takes the oath of office as first President at Federal Hall in New York City on April 30, 1789. Although he had selected the site for the White House and approved its design, he never lived there.

While the government remained in New York, the remodeled City Hall provided space for Congress, and the first Chief Executive lived in rented houses. A handsome Georgian residence intended for President and Mrs. Washington was unfinished when the move to Philadelphia took place in 1790; once there the President occupied a house owned by Robert Morris.

For the permanent buildings in the "Federal City"—as he modestly called it—Washington wanted "size, form, and elegance" looking "beyond the present day." But for early use, he thought, builders should put up an Executive Mansion suited to the time, and leave anything more to the future when the country would surely be richer, larger, more populous, and more important in the world. In 1793, a year after the Dublin-trained builder James Hoban won a medal and the commission to erect the President's House, Washington suggested that he omit a third story.

Although Washington generously called the assorted designs submitted a credit to architecture in an infant republic, most of them were more gallant than skilled. Hoban's design (see pages 108-9) stood out in competence, originality, and practicality—he included a plan, eventually discarded, for wings to be added when necessary. His unusual "elliptic saloon," today the Blue Room, has drawn admiring comment for generations.

In supervising construction, Hoban met varied and complex frustrations, as did his counterpart Dr. William Thornton, who was struggling to get the Capitol ready. Skilled hands for such enterprises were few; free workmen apparently avoided an area where slave labor kept wages low. Sales of lots in the District of Columbia lagged. Congress economized on appropriations. Materials brought by water came slowly upriver as wind and tide favored the ships.

By June 1800, when 131 federal employees arrived with their accumulated papers and President John Adams came to visit a city of 501 households, neither the "Congress house" nor the "President's Palace" was complete. Thinking that one man could certainly find lodging somewhere, the harried commissioners had stopped work on the "Palace" the year before to concentrate on the Capitol. Its north wing was available when legislators straggled into town in November, and Adams found shelter if not comfort at the mansion.

His wife, Abigail, during the first weeks of occupancy, penned candid letters to her daughter, listing the problems of a house on such "a grand and superb scale." Not a single bell to summon a servant— officials had scrabbled desperately to procure these, without success. No firewood, in a region of forests—"because people cannot be found to cut and cart it!"—and raw winter weather. Of the six rooms she called "comfortable" and described, none was her own. With some justice she thought New Englanders would have done a better job of finishing things. Meanwhile, she warned, her daughter should keep all these

During his term of office, President and Mrs. Washington lived in this Philadelphia house (right) owned by financier Robert Morris. When New York was the capital, they first occupied a brick house on Cherry Street, then a residence on Broadway. In both cities, houses built for the President were completed too late for the Washingtons to use. Time-darkened silver of the Chippendale looking glass below reflected the Washingtons while they stayed in the Morris home.

ORIGINAL WATERCOLOR BY W. L. BRETON, HISTORICAL SOCIETY OF PENNSYLVANIA

Gilbert Stuart based this portrait of Abigail Adams (left) on a study he made when she was First Lady. She and her husband, John, became the first residents of the White House in November 1800. The graceful Sheffield coffee urn (below), which bears their initials, was one of their most prized possessions.

COURTESY OF THE NATIONAL GALLERY OF ART; WHITE HOUSE COLLECTION (RIGHT)

*Final design for the
President's House (above)
was drawn in 1793
by Irish architect
James Hoban. He added
an American eagle in
the pediment to such
traditional features
as a hipped roof,
balustrade, and arches
alternating with
triangles above the
windows. Another effort
in the same style appears
at lower left, a design
submitted by James
Diamond of Maryland.
The sophisticated plan
above it, inscribed
only "A. Z.," is
thought to be the work*

of Thomas Jefferson.
He turned to Italian
Renaissance architect
Andrea Palladio for
inspiration; others
followed such designs
as that at right center
from James Gibbs's 1728
Book of Architecture,
the most popular
builder's guide of the
18th century. Its idiom
survives in Irish
mansions like Leinster
House (upper right)
and at the Château de
Rastignac in southwest
France, where an oval
portico resembles the
one Hoban added to the
White House in 1824.

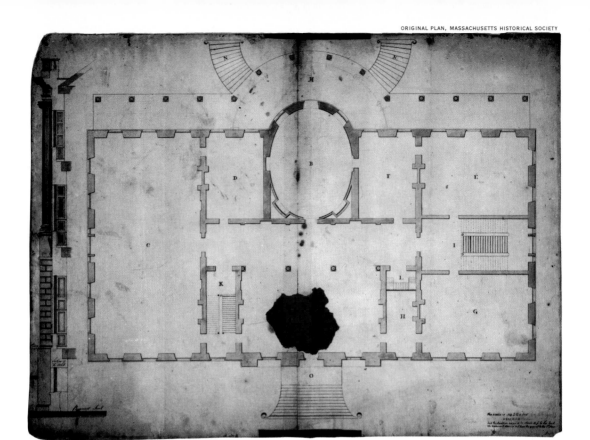

James Hoban, architect and builder of the White House, drew the plan for the State Floor (above) in his bid for the commission. It includes a portico and a colonnade that was never constructed.

complaints secret and quote her as saying only that "the situation is beautiful, which is true."

Undoubtedly Mrs. Adams meant the general vicinity, since the grounds of the mansion were a disreputable jumble of old kilns and water-filled pits for brickmaking, stonecutters' shacks, sheds for supplies, rubbish, and mud.

On November 15 the commissioners hired one James Clarke to get the back stairs and a privy built within a fortnight, and then to complete the interior doors and the grand window at the east end of the house. Evidently, when the lady of the White House had laundry hung up to dry in the East Room, it flapped in winter winds.

According to an inventory taken February 26, 1801, the Adamses had a fair amount of furniture at their disposal. The President's bed had white dimity curtains; his "dressing" mirror was "in tolerable order." Solid silver plate included two large "punch urns" with ladles and five dozen teaspoons; 33 pairs of sheets were "generally good," three "Table setts" of china complete. And the stables housed an "Elegant Chariot," a "Good Coachee," a "Market Waggon," and "7 Well looking Horses, chiefly advanced in years."

After four months of shivering in their chilly "castle," offering the most ceremonious hospitality possible under the circumstances, after weeks of uncertainty before the House of Representatives settled an electoral tie between Thomas Jefferson and Aaron Burr for President,

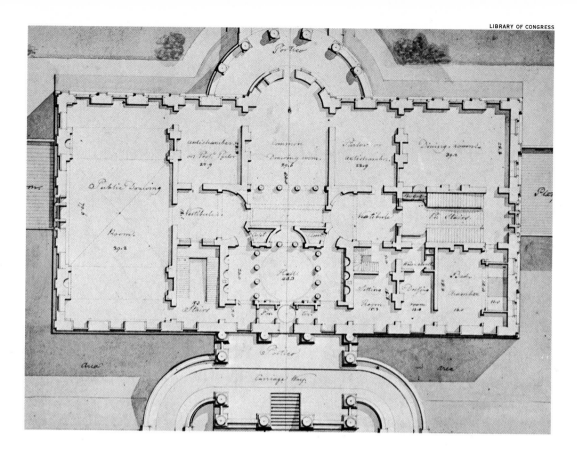

the first residents of the White House were free to leave Washington.

An unfinished house was unlikely to annoy Jefferson, who had happily spent years remodeling Monticello, but he waited until March 19 before moving from a boardinghouse near the Capitol into his sandstone mansion. Then, as the first President to spend a full term there, he began his efforts to improve it and furnish it in style. The worst of the junk was carted out of the grounds and a post-and-rail fence erected. Instead of finding their way up wooden steps to the oval room that had been serving as a vestibule, guests picked their way up wooden steps to the north entrance. The principal staircase inside the mansion was not completed until the middle of Jefferson's first term.

In 1803, amateur architect Jefferson appointed professional architect Benjamin Henry Latrobe "Surveyor of the Public Buildings," and soon Latrobe was planning a new roof for the White House. So much rainwater had leaked through that the ceiling of the East Room had collapsed. Under the load of ill-fitting slates, the front and back walls of the mansion had started to spread. Latrobe substituted sheet iron, sparing the structure an estimated 82 tons, and secured the walls "by strong ties of Iron."

To provide a formal entryway from the north, in 1807 Latrobe built a platform with a strong vaulted support bridging the deep areaway that gave light to basement kitchens on this side of the mansion. Underneath the porch, vendors rolled up to the kitchen door to deliver food

English-born architect Benjamin Henry Latrobe submitted the above plan to Jefferson in 1807. It proposed porticoes as well as a modification of rooms on the State Floor that was never executed.

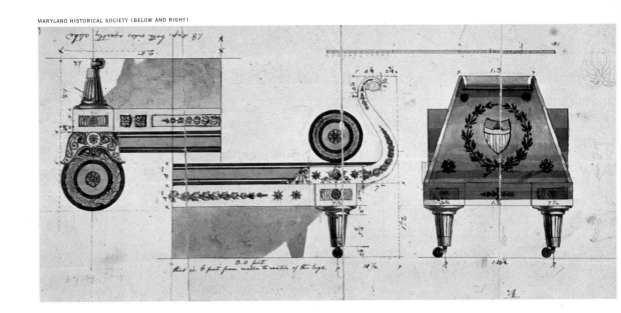

Latrobe, named Surveyor of the Public Buildings by Jefferson in 1803, not only made changes on the exterior of the White House but also designed furniture for it. His drawing of the south facade (lower right) included pavilions and terraces completed in 1808. Latrobe's rendering of the east elevation shows the North Portico, finished in 1830, and the South Portico, completed in 1824. Latrobe began his collaboration in 1809 with the new

lady of the mansion, Dolley Madison, to decorate the "Oval Drawing Room" (today's Blue Room) in classical-revival style. He based the 36 painted and gilded cane-seat chairs on the klismos—a chair of Greek design; he adapted the triclinium—a couch used by Romans for reclining at meals—for two sofas and four window seats (above left). All were lost when the British burned the mansion on August 24, 1814.

and household goods to the steward. A year later, to conceal household and office space, Jefferson designed low-lying pavilions east and west of the mansion; Latrobe completed these in 1808, including a fireproof vault for the Treasury at the far end of the East Colonnade.

Although Jefferson's modifications to the White House progressed slowly, his changes in Presidential etiquette began in March 1801. Washington and Adams had favored a stately formality in the 18th-century mold of public dignity, praised by their admirers as upholding the greatness of America and denounced by their critics as savoring of monarchy. President Jefferson introduced a dramatic informality, acclaimed by his followers as true to the genius of the republic and scorned by his enemies as cheap in the debased fashion of French radicals. He sometimes greeted visitors in his slippers; he seated no one by precedence at his dinners—but if this infuriated diplomats, it cost few votes. Between these extremes, subsequent Presidents have adapted the usage of the White House to the changing customs of the country, while the public watched their restoration of a seemly order or their innovations toward a welcome ease.

For all his democratic manners, Jefferson furnished the White House in sophisticated style. He liked furniture "in the antique taste"—the classical revival manner with the crisp lines and cool restraint represented in France by the style now designated Louis XVI and in America by the term Federal. An inventory of 1809 distinguished mahogany pieces from the "fashionable" ones, with gilding and paint in crimson, green, blue, or black. Jefferson ignored precedent by draping many windows not in damask or brocade but in fashionable bright chintz. Unfortunately, it seems that none of his many guests—no artist, no drawing master, no cultivated person—so much as sketched any of his rooms or furnishings.

Fire-darkened and crumbling, the White House stands desolate in 1816, beyond St. John's Church (also designed by Latrobe). The Madisons spent the last of his term in rented quarters—first Col. John Tayloe's Octagon House, then a smaller residence nearby.

When that incomparable hostess Dolley Madison undertook to redecorate the mansion shortly after her husband's inauguration in 1809, she asked Latrobe to design furniture for the "Oval Drawing Room." He drew chairs "to a Grecian Model," with sofas and settees "to match the same." They were made by John and Hugh Finlay of Baltimore. Latrobe's drawings survive (pages 112-13), and their muted tints help explain his wail of anguish when he saw the crimson velvet bought for cushions and draperies: "The curtains! Oh the terrible velvet curtains! Their effect will ruin me entirely so brilliant will they be."

In fact the room seemed entirely elegant when the Madisons received callers there on New Year's Day, 1810; contemporary accounts praised it highly. In 1813 young Elbridge Gerry, Jr., son of the Vice President, found it "immense and magnificent"; its curtains—"which cost 4$ a yard"—struck him as "superb."

This elegance was short-lived; barely a year later the British burned the White House. On August 23, while the President was off with an ill-trained army, Mrs. Madison packed a carriage load of Cabinet papers

*This writing arm Windsor chair was used by Madison on the night
of August 26, 1814, as he sat dispatching messages to his Cabinet from
the Quaker town of Brookeville, Maryland. His medicine chest was
taken from the mansion by a British soldier; a Canadian descendant
returned it in 1939. A tea box from 1811, acquired in 1971,
contains wallpaper ascribed by descendants of Latrobe to "the drawing
room of the President's House."*

FRANKLIN D. ROOSEVELT LIBRARY,
HYDE PARK, NEW YORK

WHITE HOUSE COLLECTION

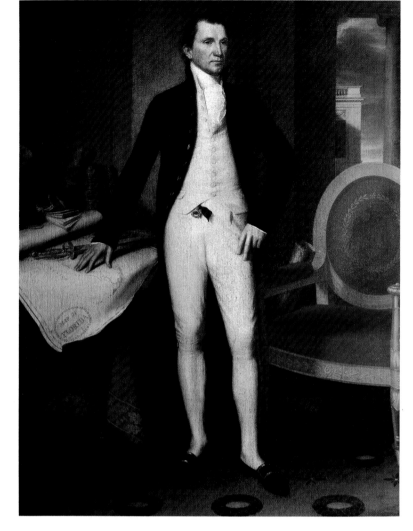

*His official home
restored, James Monroe
stands by one of
the 38 chairs made
in 1817 for the oval
drawing room by Pierre-
Antoine Bellangé of
Paris, cabinetmaker to
the rulers of France.
A superb pier table from
the same group, adorned
with carved and gilded
branches of olive, now
stands in the Entrance
Hall; it never left the
mansion. Baroness Hyde
de Neuville, wife of
the French Minister,
sketched an 1820 view
of the White House with
its neighboring office
buildings (below).
From left: Departments
of State, Treasury,
War, and Navy.*

*By 1848 gas lamps lit Pennsylvania Avenue in front of the White House, as
shown in a lithograph (above) based on a watercolor by Augustus Köllner.
This scene, entitled "President's House," depicts the view from Lafayette Square.*

into trunks; the next day she continued a letter to her sister, writing "within sound of the cannon! Mr. Madison comes not; may God protect him!" Someone procured a wagon; she ordered the government's silver put into it. She insisted on taking "the large picture of Gen. Washington. . . . I have ordered the frame to be broken, and the canvas taken out; it is done. . . . When I shall again write to you, or where I shall be tomorrow, I cannot tell!!" That night, August 24, the flames of the blazing mansion and Capitol raged against the sky until a summer downpour quenched them, leaving the dank smell of burned ruin.

Even after the treaty of peace, Washingtonians feared that Congress might decide to move the Capital to some safer place; and when the decision to remain was clear, rebuilding for the legislature took priority. The Madisons lived for a year in Col. John Tayloe's mansion, Octagon House, then in a smaller house on Pennsylvania Avenue.

Hoban took charge of his crumbling mansion, stripping out fire-damaged stone and brick and rebuilding the exterior walls. By mid-September 1817 the White House was habitable again, and Congress had appropriated $20,000 for furnishings alone. James Monroe had acquired valuable Louis XVI furniture as a diplomat in Paris; he sold this, with china and plate, to the government—and his agent muddled the transactions so badly that the matter was never fully untangled. To supplement his private collection and some used items of good quality that had been bought for the Madisons, Monroe ordered an array of goods from France for the oval drawing room, a parlor, a card room, and the dining room. He also bought American furniture; William King of Georgetown charged $1,584 in one bill for 24 chairs (one pictured opposite) and four sofas.

Filled with patriotic pride and curiosity, a throng arrived on January 1, 1818, to see the President's House in its new splendor. In the oval room where the Chief Magistrate stood, gilded Empire furniture from Bellangé of Paris (see pages 46-47, 50, 51) shone in light playing from the hearth and the 50-candle chandelier. Ornaments of porcelain and silver, vermeil and gilded bronze (see pages 36, 59) glittered on mantels and tables; on fine silks the sheen was still undimmed.

From that day to this, items from the Monroe restoration have formed the heart of the historic collection of the White House—with the one treasured exception known to have belonged to the mansion since 1800: the Gilbert Stuart portrait of George Washington (see page 37) that Dolley Madison rescued from looting or destruction. One piece of the Bellangé furniture never left the collection—the pier table now in the Entrance Hall. But as recently as 1960, the remainder of the suite and most of Monroe's American pieces seemed beyond retrieving.

Throughout the 19th century, the residents of the White House furnished it in the current style whenever possible. They wanted the fashionable, the up-to-date, the modern, the changing finery of a fast-changing country. They made the best of what they inherited from

French artistry, 1817: one of a pair of fruit baskets wrought in bronze-doré. Bought for the dining room, each arrived with detachable branches to hold six candles.

former administrations, and thriftily, matter-of-factly, sold it at public auction as it grew outmoded and worn.

Yellowing accounts indicate some of the sums realized this way; but what became of which piece of furniture, at which sale and when, is seldom a matter of record.

Appropriations to keep the White House presentable were routine if not adequate, but a President with substantial opposition in Congress could expect trouble over household issues. Opponents of John Adams kicked up trouble with charges that he bought his seven "Well looking Horses" with money earmarked for furniture. His son John Quincy Adams, elected in 1824 with a minority of the popular vote, met a similar fuss over the private purchase of a billiard table and never did succeed in getting money enough to furnish the East Room.

And White House furnishings take hard wear, if not downright abuse. From one administration to the next, superb velvet curtains, elegant green silks, rich handwoven carpets pass from the freshness of a New Year's Day to the terse judgments of the man taking inventory: "in tolerable order . . . injured . . . more than half worn . . . much worn . . ." to the final "worn out." By March 24, 1825, a clerk reported that Monroe's purchases, "having been seven years or upwards, in use," were "of necessity more or less injured and defaced, notwithstanding the utmost care and attention. . . ." The portion collected for the Madisons in 1814 had become "altogether useless."

Not only changes in usefulness but also changes in equipment for American households—changes in technology and standards of comfort—come to life in White House records. The 1825 survey finds in a private room "one set yellow silk dome bed curtains" for "one elegant mahogany gilt mounted bedstead" with "one husk mattress"—the delicate sibilance of silk is answered in the harsher rustle of cornshucks.

Local artistry, 1818: one of 24 chairs that Monroe bought for the East Room from William King, cabinetmaker of Georgetown.

Much louder but with a similar change of key, the inauguration of Andrew Jackson spoke of a triumph for the frontier and political democracy. "Old Hickory," Hero of New Orleans, commanded the admiration of citizens with no time for polish—or veneer—and persons of gentility feared the mob would reign.

In fact, Jackson took pains to embellish the Executive Mansion. Long-deferred work on the North Portico got under way at once. For the first time a President was in a position to furnish the East Room; it was promptly done. To replace glass chipped and shattered since 1817, a Pittsburgh firm supplied a copious shipment costing $1,451.75 which included 12 dozen "richest cut" tumblers and 18 dozen wineglasses. A French porcelain dinner service of 440 pieces and a dessert set of 412 pieces came to $2,500. After eight years of high-toned entertaining and full-throated politics, General Jackson retired, still a popular hero.

His protégé Martin Van Buren had the bad luck to face not just a

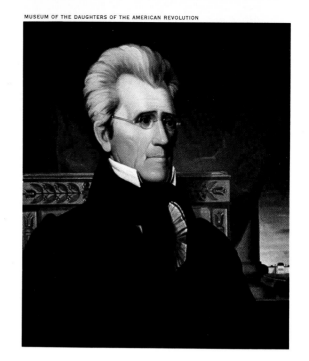

President Andrew Jackson, portrayed by Ralph Earl, sits with stiff dignity in one of the Bellangé chairs. Like Jefferson, Jackson lived by a standard of ease and elegance that never cost him popular support. At far right, a print by Robert Cruikshank caricatures the crowd at a Jackson reception as "President's Levee, or all Creation going to the White-house, Washington." By Jackson's time the reception rooms were jammed even on routine occasions; the local population was passing 30,000. Below, a detail of George Cooke's 1833 painting shows Washington from across the Anacostia River.

financial panic and the worst depression the country had suffered to date, but the canniest Congressman who ever made fun of White House furbelows. On April 14, 1840, Representative Charles Ogle of Pennsylvania rose in the House to attack the "regal splendor of the Presidential palace." The President was a Democrat, Ogle a Whig. With appropriations acts, bills, and vouchers for evidence, he lambasted details from dwarf walls on the grounds to "ice cream vases" and bracket lights. Deftly he implied that other Presidents' purchases were Van Buren's doing. Ogle made great play with the satin medallion and galloon and gimp at windows in the "Blue Elliptical Saloon." After presenting Van Buren as a sissified spendthrift, he ridiculed him as a skinflint, making the plain farmers, poor laborers, and honest mechanics of America pay for cobweb brushes, churn and milk strainers, and the hemming of 12 dozen dishrags at the "pitiful price" of 50 cents per dozen.

Van Buren had spent less than Jackson. Even a few Whigs pointed out distortions in Ogle's ruthless comedy. Van Buren lost the election.

On a storm tide of hard cider and ballyhoo, William Henry Harrison won the Presidency, began his purchases for the mansion, took the oath of office, fell ill within a month, and died. The first President to die in office, he left his running mate John Tyler to take up the burdens of the executive branch with minimal support in Cabinet and Congress. As the latter refused Tyler's plea for additional funds for the White House, its furnishings rapidly approached dilapidation.

Upholstered only once since 1817, the chairs reached a condition of "perfect explosion at every prominent point that presents contact with the outer garments of the visitors." Those in the East Room, said one journal, would disgrace a house of shame.

I n 1845, the James K. Polks' first year in the mansion, money for furnishings became available again. Victorian fancy took charge—walnut frames, purple plush, rockers in green figured plush for the Red Room, 24 "Gothic" chairs—an early instance of the vogue for revivals that pilfered the styles of various ages in rapid succession.

New amenities appeared: payment of $25 for a "Refregrator" (icebox) was authorized in 1845; gas lights were installed in 1848. Older amenities were maintained. On June 30, 1849, early in President Zachary Taylor's term, someone fitted a carpet in the water closet, charging 50 cents. An attic cistern for rainwater had supplied a water closet in Jefferson's time; running water from a city system dated only from Jackson's.

Although Hoban had added 12 new fireplaces in 1817 and Van Buren had installed a furnace, heating remained a problem. Franklin Pierce had the benefit not only of a bathroom but also of an improved heating plant to make the mansion more comfortable.

Perhaps no President was better suited to preside comfortably at the Executive Mansion than James Buchanan, the dignified bachelor

In "The Republican Court in the Days of Lincoln," a group portrait by Peter F. Rothermel, Civil War dignitaries are easily identifiable: Gen. Ulysses S. Grant appears to the left of President Lincoln; Mrs. Lincoln bends to speak to Gen. Winfield Scott, seated at right. Costly fabrics chosen by Mary Lincoln for the mansion were damaged during the war years, when visitors cut or tore souvenirs from furniture, draperies, and even rugs.

who once described himself as "an old public functionary." With the poised help of his niece Harriet Lane, who acted as hostess, he entertained often and genially. In 1857 Congress allotted $5,000 to buy portraits of five former Presidents, plus a routine $20,000 that paid for a new conservatory. For the Blue Room, where Monroe's furniture had stood since 1817, he ordered a rococo-revival suite that served for decades (pages 126-27); except for the large pier table, the Bellangé pieces were sold at auction.

With veteran aplomb Buchanan welcomed the first envoys from Japan; in the autumn of 1860 he received Queen Victoria's heir, Prince Edward, traveling for diplomatic reasons under the title of Baron Renfrew. The first royal houseguest made a great impression—for years thereafter people spoke of the "Prince of Wales room." (Today this room serves as the President's private dining room.)

Probably no President ever faced a crisis for which his abilities were less suited than Buchanan. The sectional dreads and suspicions that had challenged Monroe's tact, Jackson's fire, (Continued on page 128)

Photograph of the East Room (above), taken soon after the Civil War, shows the King chairs, Jackson's chandeliers— converted to gas—and ceiling decorations from 1853. Grant's redecoration in 1873 (below) resulted in decor hailed at the time as "pure Greek" but later ridiculed as "steamboat Gothic."

The stars and stripes deck the East Room for the Army and Navy Reception of 1900, when

their Commander in Chief received high-ranking military officers at
this annual White House event. Two years later the opulent Victorian
decor gave way to Colonial revival. Today Gilbert Stuart's portrait
of Washington, to the left of the fireplace, hangs again in the room.

*In the Blue Room of the early 1870's (above), decorated by President
Andrew Johnson's daughter Martha Johnson Patterson, geometrical
forms accent the contour of Hoban's "elliptic saloon." The rococo-
revival furniture dates from the Buchanan Administration. Mrs.
Patterson chose the blue paper with panels bordered in black and gold.
On New Year's Day, 1867, when the refurbished parlor first went on
show at the traditional public levee, the weather was "most inclement";
muslin covers protected the velvet carpets. Two decades later, during
Cleveland's first term, the room (right) contains Louis C. Tiffany's
decor, introduced by President Arthur. A shield-and-star pattern
replaces the sweeping ovals of the ceiling. The delicate robin's egg tint
of the hand-pressed wallpaper was accented in ivory; in the rosettes
sparkled inlay of opaque or colored glass. From the mantel, below
Monroe's vases and clock, hangs a new adornment: velvet fringe.*

Taylor's stern obstinacy, and Fillmore's conciliation, increased during Buchanan's term and neared flash point with the election of Lincoln.

When the Lincolns moved into the White House, a tough group of Kansans joined Senator Jim Lane as "Frontier Guards," to patrol the porticoes with muskets, and drill or sleep in the East Room until loyal troops arrived to defend the Capital. "A sort of uncanny glamour seems to have been settling upon the city. . . ," wrote one of Lincoln's secretaries; "a strange and shuddering kind of thing, and its central, darkest, most bewildering witchcraft works around this Executive Mansion."

Whatever uncertainties hovered around it, Mary Lincoln meant to hold her own there and make it home. She put warm sheepskin rugs by the beds. Inevitably, visitors were finding the furniture "deplorably shabby." She selected new rosewood furniture, new velvet hassocks, new plush and brocatelle fabrics. She overran an appropriation by $6,700; the responsible official endorsed a wallpaper bill for the state floor *"as selected by Mrs. Lincoln & not by Com. Pub. Bdgs."*

Angrily Lincoln refused to ask for a deficiency appropriation: ". . . it would stink in the nostrils of the American people to have it said that the President of the United States had approved a bill overrunning an appropriation of $20 000 for *flub dubs* for this damned old house, when the soldiers cannot have blankets."

In former decades, foreigners had remarked that plain citizens at the White House controlled themselves with self-respecting good manners. However, a kind of hysterical vandalism marked the war years. A man was caught "skinning" satin damask from a sofa. Even as Congress was enacting deficiency bills for the mansion, its finery suffered.

Word-of-mouth tradition was keeping up with the mansion's heirlooms, more or less. Lincoln's secretary William O. Stoddard remembered the piece known as "Andrew Jackson's chair," presented to him

Lincoln's office and Cabinet Room as of October 1864: a detailed and invaluable sketch by C. K. Stellwagen. He noted that Lincoln's chair by the window was covered in black haircloth. Littering the Cabinet table are maps, books, and rolls of documents, including long letters endorsing many a plea for military rank or civil office. In a sketch published in 1877, office seekers crowd the mansion to see newly inaugurated President Rutherford B. Hayes.

by citizens of Mexico. A "unique mahogany frame" and "hollow morocco leather seat" made it "peculiarly comfortable." Legend had it that Jackson leaned back in it on winter evenings before the fireplace in his room, smoking his pipe and resting his stockinged feet on the middle bricks of the fireplace arch. "Mr. Lincoln expressed a wish to have those bricks preserved when the fireplace was reconstructed, but they were somehow mislaid and lost."

As for physical change, Lincoln made only a minor one, long since eliminated: a private passage on the second floor from the library through the reception room to his office. (Today it would run from the Yellow Oval Room through the President's Office to the Lincoln Bedroom.) Thus he could reach the private quarters unseen by waiting strangers. A contemporary called it ". . . his only monument in the building . . . it tells a long story of duns and loiterers, contract-hunters and seekers for commissions, garrulous parents on paltry errands, toadies without measure and talkers without conscience."

Nasty eddies of bitterness followed the widowed Mary Lincoln from the mansion: charges that she had taken away public property. Indignantly she itemized things she had packed, gifts from humble Unionists: waxwork, country quilts, homemade chairs. Apparently no one really supervised the White House during the five weeks she lay mourning in her room, and vandals helped themselves. With official approval she had taken a shaving stand her husband had liked, leaving one of equal quality to replace it.

President Andrew Johnson, for all his troubles with Congress, received funds to decorate the house again, and President Ulysses S. Grant carried out a thorough renovation in 1873, at the height of the Gilded Age. Splendor aside, by now the White House was showing its years in ominous fashion. The Commissioner of Public Buildings

Exotica and domestic luxury meet in the Harrisons' Red Room (left), the family parlor; a Tiffany mantel with tortoiseshell tiles; an Austrian firescreen; Oriental vases and screens; crimson wallpaper with a "Moorish" frieze. In 1882 President Arthur had called on Louis Tiffany of New York to redecorate the mansion in the emerging style of Art Nouveau. The most famous installation was the stained-glass screen in the Cross Hall (below).

reported that a large ceiling had collapsed, "but fortunately when the room was unoccupied." Almost all the ceilings were cracked, and those in the state rooms had settled several inches. The basement he dismissed as "necessarily very damp and unhealthy."

He dwelt on the inconvenience of rigging up bridges from windows (page 138) when large receptions made it necessary to supplement the single entrance at the North Portico.

Closets, he noted, were "now considered indispensable," and the White House had none. (Nobody built closets in the 1790's, but the age of machinery—with its textile factories and sewing machines—had left chests inadequate for the greater quantities of apparel.) Counting the library, only eight rooms were available in the private quarters for family and guests. Everything considered, the commissioner thought "it hardly seems possible to state anything in favor of the house as a residence; but if 'thoroughly repaired,' it would serve its purpose admirably as an executive office."

Of course the White House continued, however clumsily, to serve both purposes at once. If national sentiment was the only factor to assure this, it was more than enough. A President with a small family, like Grover Cleveland, could count himself lucky, but nothing could be expected to shrink the volume of public business.

The callers who sought postal or military commissions from Lincoln were replaced by callers who sought pardons from Andrew Johnson or friendly agreements with Grant, and the paperwork never diminished. Arrangements for Reconstruction in the South and for fast-growing settlements in the West were increasing the number of government jobs, the scope of patronage, the hopeful ranks of applicants. Lobbyists —even a few soft-spoken women—moved suavely among the throng on the second floor, to speak in the interest of railroads or farmers, veterans or freedmen.

From deadlock in the national life to a note on the Red Room—so crisis dwindles when successfully outlived. Unique among Presidential elections, that of 1876 strained the Constitution to the point of frantic improvising. Democrat Samuel J. Tilden apparently edged ahead of Republican Rutherford B. Hayes in popular votes, with contested electoral votes in Oregon and three southern states. One of those electoral votes could put Tilden in the White House. Behind the scenes, Northerners and Southerners were bargaining. Congress named a special Electoral Commission. As a final complication, the lawful inauguration day—March 4—fell on a Sunday, and tradition deferred the ceremonies to Monday.

On February 20, 1877, Grant assumed the count was virtually settled. He invited the Hayeses to come to the mansion as guests on March 3. "Sinister rumors from W. [Washington] leave us in doubt. . . ," Hayes replied; they planned to stay with friends but would come to dinner— if declared successful. He was, by one vote, but apprehension of some kind of coup d'etat or violence still ran high.

American eagle decorates a plate of the Harrison china, made in Limoges, France.

Grant thought Hayes should take the oath of office in secret on Saturday, just in case. Reluctantly, Hayes agreed.

As guests assembled for a dinner of surpassing brilliance, Grant quietly slipped into the Red Room with Hayes and Chief Justice Morrison R. Waite. The oath administered, they quickly returned.

On Monday, amid swirls of rumor about the oath but no violence whatever, the public ceremonies took place with as much decorum as ever. Reporters fell back on the decor of the red parlor for mood or detail. "Its crimson fires fell upon them . . ." cried one; "Red mirrors of a darker red reflected the smouldering light of other mirrors. . . . a dark blood flush, enveloped them. . . . the consecrated and the priest went out together to the sound of merriment . . . the flash of gems in women's ears and the beards of o'erambitious men."

The room is "between the banquet hall and the violet blue Parlor," noted another journalist, and was newly furnished in "the English version of the Queen Anne." The Japanese Minister had presented two small Japanese cabinets. The writer faithfully described the fire screen as "a curious large gilt one with a worsted center piece," but did not mention that Austria was the donor.

In 1878 Hayes accepted the credentials of the first Chinese minister to the United States, in a private ceremony in the Blue Room. The Imperial diplomats wore their national costume, which always attracted attention at state dinners.

Of international gifts, probably none has given longer service than the desk presented to President Hayes, a token of goodwill from Great Britain. In 1854 the crew of H.M.S. *Resolute,* trapped in Arctic ice, had abandoned her; the Yankee whaler *George Henry* in 1855 freed the *Resolute* and brought her to port. The ship was bought, refitted, and given to Queen Victoria by President Pierce on behalf of the American people. Two decades later, the *Resolute* was broken up and Her Majesty had the desk made from the old ship's seasoned oak. Since then many Presidents have used it in their private studies or the Oval Office.

The White House staff—like the diplomatic corps—was growing. In 1881 a de facto "Bureau of Appointments"—seven persons counting the President's private secretary—had second-floor office space to cope with patronage demands raining down on James A. Garfield. That same year the shooting of the President by a disappointed office seeker brought demands for reform and led to establishment of the Civil Service in 1883.

Chester A. Arthur, whose urbane New York ways earned him the nickname "Elegant Arthur," inherited an Executive Mansion not at all to his taste. One nostalgic visitor had dismissed the furnishings as "modern abominations in upholstery and garish gilding" and the rooms as "staring, pretentious and Frenchy," preferring the quiet dignity of Lincoln's mahogany pieces in their port-wine plush. Arthur swept out innumerable abominations on April 15, 1882—24 wagonloads, by report, for the greatest "decayed furnishings" auction in White House annals. A crowd of 5,000 bid high for moth-eaten furniture from

Mrs. Benjamin Harrison, an avid painter of china, helped design the state service during her husband's administration. She also initiated the tradition of collecting state and family china of previous Presidents. Vast amounts of china were necessary for state dinners like the one below during the administration of Grover Cleveland. Meals often included 10 to 15 courses.

At the height of fashion: a
guest bedroom in the Benjamin
Harrison Administration. The
"Lincoln" bed keeps its
original cornice of gilt wood,
with crown drapery of lace
and fringed curtains. The
marble-top center table was
purchased with the bed, and
the chairs beside the table
probably were acquired at
the same time. These, from a
set of six, stood in a guest
room during Andrew Johnson's
term. Possibly the same
order included the chaise, or
daybed, veiled by its afghan
and dust ruffles. The massive
wardrobe with mirrored doors
was probably bought by
Buchanan or Lincoln because
the house had no closets;
the shallow case beside it with
a flowered curtain was fitted
with exercise equipment. In this
and many other pictures,
Frances Benjamin Johnston—
one of the first women to win
fame as a news photographer—
compiled a unique record of
the White House in the 1890's.
Here she caught not only the
period's fondness for pattern
upon pattern, but also the
mansion's typical mixture of
the stately and the purely
personal: the grandeur
of the antique bed, a homely
crocheted pillowcase.

Expansion for an overcrowded house: With Mrs. Benjamin Harrison's encouragement, architect Fred D. Owen produced the first definite plans for enlarging the Executive Mansion. An immense new greenhouse extended across the south grounds in his most extravagant scheme (top). Cleveland's proposal of 1896 also included two large wings, but related them more successfully to the historic house. McKinley's 1900 model presents cupolas—an idea borrowed from the original wings of the Capitol.

the East Room, hair mattresses, marble mantels, curtains, matting, carpets, cuspidors, and an old globe of the world that once belonged to President Grant's daughter Nellie.

Along with assorted repairs to modernize the mansion, Arthur called in the famous Louis C. Tiffany of New York to redecorate the state rooms in a manner that foreshadowed Art Nouveau. He found little to do in the East Room but adorn the ceiling with silver and tones of ivory; his famous stained-glass screen (pages 130-31) in the Entrance Hall, now known only by black-and-white photographs, interlaced American eagles and flags "in the Arabian method."

None of Tiffany's major contributions were altered for Mrs. Cleveland in 1886. New lace curtains, fresh paint, touches of regilding, and diligent cleaning prepared the residence for the bride of the only President to marry in the mansion. In January 1887 she held her first reception and the first of her Saturday afternoon levees to let working women meet the Lady of the White House as women of society were free to do. (Only after 1900 did the term "First Lady" come into general use.)

Just how President Benjamin Harrison fitted his family into five bedrooms taxes imagination and record. It included his wife, her 90-year-old father, her sister and then a niece; son Russell, his wife, their daughter; daughter Mary McKee, two infants. Mrs. Harrison soon began a campaign for enlarging and improving the White House.

She ordered mold caused by faulty plumbing scrubbed off old walls, had layers of rotting floorboards peeled out of ground-floor rooms, and settled down to her hobby of painting china. She decorated cracker boxes, flowerpot saucers, and chocolate jugs—the greenhouses provided azaleas and orchids to copy. Her investigation of an old china closet led to the White House china collection, which represents almost every President through Lyndon B. Johnson and now contains pieces from the service added by Ronald Reagan.

Her interest in history inspired the idea of a "Historical Art Wing" for the enlarged mansion, but that project perished in the wake of a spat over patronage. The mansion was refurbished, with 30-inch-deep panels of blue glass decorated with gold scrollwork at the top of the Blue Room windows. Harrison found the new rooms "much improved," but wrote that the "greatest beauty of all" was in the bathroom "with the white tile and marble and porcelain-lined tub. They would tempt a duck to wash himself every day."

What Americans liked in the late 19th century, generally speaking, probably shows most vividly in the Harrisons' rooms (pages 134-35): the comfort of abundance in figured wallpaper, figured carpets, figured upholstery, tassels and fringe, furniture with curlicues cut by jigsaw, would-be Turkish cushions. An age enchanted by prosperity found the American furniture made about 1800 plain to the point of indecency.

Elaboration reached its zenith and by the McKinley Administration had begun to recede. Panels in the Blue Room evoked the simpler decor

In the grounds of the White House, the century between 1802 and 1902 brought impressive change. Just when the first greenhouse on the east side appeared is uncertain, but documentary evidence places one on the west grounds in 1857. By 1900 greenhouses (above) to supply the mansion with cut flowers and potted plants had spread west and south of the house. The official in charge, Col. Theodore A. Bingham, fought in vain to save a camellia house in 1902. For most of the 1800's the North Portico provided the principal

door for guests; as early
as President John Tyler's
term, large crowds
departed by way of
improvised bridges (left)
at windows—usually set
up outside the East
Room. Finally in 1902
a major renovation
added an entrance at
the east, swept away
all the greenhouses, and
erected the temporary
West Wing of offices
(above). The classic lines
of the south façade
contrast vividly with
the ornament of a
Victorian gatehouse
probably from the 1870's
—and with the plain
little house for the
guard dog (right).

of the Louis XVI style. With pale carpeting and walls, white counterpanes on thin-railed brass beds, and a chaise lounge and comfortable chairs upholstered in white, the McKinleys' northwest bedroom was light and airy. From the chandelier, a wire trailed down to the white-ruffled electric lamp on the table below. (The Harrisons had been wary of the intricate, patched-together electrical system.) But Victoriana still reigned through most of the State Floor.

Like Cleveland's effort to get the White House enlarged, McKinley's failed. As the centennial of the Capital drew near, a movement developed with the dream of restoring the city to meet the visions of George Washington and the plans drawn by Pierre Charles L'Enfant. Many agreed with architect Glenn Brown that the mansion should also be enlarged and restored to this historic ideal.

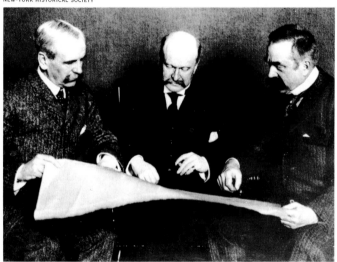

Architects of the 1902 renovation and expansion of the White House ordered by Theodore Roosevelt: from left, William R. Mead, Charles F. McKim, and Stanford White.

Thrust into the White House by McKinley's assassination in 1901, Theodore Roosevelt dismissed suggestions that the President might live anywhere else, agreed that he should have offices outside the house, and called in the most prominent firm of architects in the country, McKim, Mead & White, known for their work in the historic style called "Colonial." With appropriation in hand as of June 1902, T. R. insisted on an October deadline for the new offices, with more leeway for the state rooms.

They found the Ground Floor in bad condition, and most of the State Floor settling dangerously. On the second story, flooring needed total replacement. Rainwater was still channeled through the walls in hollowed-out logs; the sanitary system defied description; obsolete wiring, its insulation worn off, had charred the wooden beams; lack of safe exits made the servants' rooms in the attic potential death-traps. Working at top speed, McKim, Mead & White reconstructed the interior throughout, excavating a new basement for the heating system.

They swept away the conservatories—"Smash the glass houses!" T. R. ordered—restored Jefferson's west pavilion to lead to the new executive offices, and rebuilt the east pavilion to shelter visitors arriving at a new east entrance. (By chance, Glenn Brown—who assisted in the renovation—learned from a New Jersey architect that an east pavilion had been pulled down in 1866 and by 1900 had been generally forgotten.) They provided cloakroom space, an exasperating need since the days when Jackson's admirers hung their coats on the fence outside.

Charles McKim's painstaking decoration of the State Floor obliterated the proud luxuries of the Victorians. The East Room emerged with

East approaches, before and after: The east gate offered access to the grounds—a shortcut for pedestrians—but no entrance to the mansion suited for large gatherings until 1902. Then a portico that would hold 500 people and a porte cochere, capable of sheltering three carriages at once, came into service; an arcade in the restored pavilion led to the mansion.

Enlarged and redecorated, the State Dining Room of 1902 (above) combined the classical taste of Charles McKim and the individual preferences of Theodore Roosevelt. Wallpaper bordered with flowers and festoons gave way to fielded panels of burl oak. Trophy heads gazed blankly over reproductions of Queen Anne chairs. Doubling the seating capacity here put an end to scenes of make-do magnificence in the East Room, adorned at right for a dinner honoring Prince Henry of Prussia before alterations began. A stereoscopic view caught detail, from smilax garlands to cut glass. The makers of this "artisque coleur" stereograph, describing the scene, asserted proudly: "It must have seemed to the German prince very much like a dinner in a Christmas tree. . . ."

the aspect it keeps today. Parquet floors gleamed uncarpeted—but T. R. put a polar bear pelt in the Green Room. Along with Hayes's gaily tiled floor and Harrison's elaborate frescoes, the Tiffany screen passed into oblivion; the Entrance Hall took on the plain composure of stone. Spare, austere, consciously historic, the White House entered its second century.

Ever since 1902 an authentic look of the early years of the republic has been the ideal for those decorating the state rooms. Freewheeling incongruities vanished—such as adornments of the "Corridor" in 1898: delicate blue Venetian glass vases decorated with boars' heads, selected by Mrs. Grant; chairs made of elk antlers, from Arthur's term. When no antiques were available, reproductions served.

Although construction of the West Wing had finally ended the noisy inconveniences of a half-public second floor, the demands of a house for a nation left the private quarters none too large. Ellen Axson Wilson had attic space transformed into extra guest rooms and an artist's studio for herself; in 1927 Hoban's long-deferred third story took shape.

Hoping that the American people would help to furnish the White House, Grace Goodhue Coolidge helped persuade Congress to authorize the acceptance of appropriate antiques as gifts. A group appointed to evaluate such pieces continued to serve, under varying designations, through the Eisenhower years. Before leaving the mansion, Mrs. Coolidge had fitted out the Green Room; and she had finished crocheting a spread for the Lincoln bed, which was consigned to storage by the Tafts, brought out for the Wilsons, and sent off again by the Hardings.

President Herbert Hoover recalled from storage four of Lincoln's Cabinet chairs and grouped them with other furniture of the Lincoln-Grant era in his private study. Mrs. Hoover catalogued White House furnishings and had copies made of furniture used by the Monroes.

To Franklin and Eleanor Roosevelt, wrote one of their guests, "a chair was something to sit down on . . . a table was something to put things on and a wall was something to be covered with . . . pictures of sentimental value." Their own rooms re-created rooms at Hyde Park (though the housekeeper said the rug in Mrs. Roosevelt's room was so historic you caught your heels in it); other upstairs bedrooms had furnishings that might have come from "an old and ultrarespectable summer resort hotel" or "a W.P.A. Arts and Crafts Project." The dingiest items were replaced in 1939 during a general sprucing up to receive Their Britannic Majesties, George VI and Elizabeth, but the Roosevelts paid minimal attention to interior decorating in the midst of the Great Depression and World War II.

In 1934, rebuilding in the West Wing added a second floor and under-ground working space and repositioned the Oval Office. A new East Wing, hurriedly put up in World War II, supplied three stories of offices and the first White House bomb shelter and movie theater.

War and cold war did not keep President Harry S. Truman from taking a lively interest in the architecture of the mansion, but his controversial balcony (page 148) was hardly finished when the building gave signs of collapsing. The investigation he ordered in February 1948 grew longer as its discoveries grew more alarming; the Trumans moved into Blair House—across Pennsylvania Avenue from the White House—while architects and engineers moved into action.

Between the 1902 steel of the first floor and the 1927 steel of the third, the carrying timbers of 1817—riddled through the years by heating or ventilating flues, plumbing, and electrical conduits—were splitting under prolonged strain. "It is a wonderful thing," mused an engineer, "to contemplate the abuses that materials of construction sometimes will undergo before failure."

The architects of 1902 worked under time restrictions, those of 1927 under financial limitations. In 1949, at the President's request, Congress set up a Commission on Renovation of the Executive Mansion free of constraints. Members of the commission sensed a different necessity: to save the house as a symbol dear to Americans.

Various proposals called for demolishing the mansion completely and reproducing it with walls of granite or limestone or marble. But the old sandstone outer walls, with their broad footings and something like their original load, had survived in reasonable condition. Taking them down, as the commission felt and one member said, would be substantial and quite unnecessary desecration.

Out went furniture, chandeliers, mantelpieces from 1817 and 1902, paneling numbered and tagged for re-installation, and ornamental plasterwork—some of the sagging decorative plaster in the East Room weighed 70 pounds per square foot, but the workmen needed a jeweler's touch. Then partitions and floors were dismantled, steel shoring was installed, and the bulldozers began digging.

With concrete underpinning the old walls, a new two-story basement and new foundations, and a new steel frame, the Executive Mansion returned to life, its interior restored with fidelity. Only the main stairway changed dramatically, descending now to the Entrance Hall for additional dignity. (Continued on page 150)

Private stairway rises from the west end of the Cross Hall to the family quarters. The staircase was removed and the space added to the State Dining Room in 1902.

Raising the mansion's roof in 1927 for the construction of a new third story revealed some of the old wooden drainage system for rainwater. Crumbling ends of thick beams bore out an official warning to President Coolidge in 1923 that the roof had decayed to the point of danger. A chute at the South Portico carried down debris as crews working under tarpaulins removed second-floor ceilings, added steel girders, constructed and roofed a story of 18 rooms for storage, servants, and guests.

Fire in the West Wing on Christmas Eve, 1929, brought President Hoover from the dinner table to supervise the removal of papers from the Oval Office. Rescued items stand by a window; Mr. Hoover watches from the roof at left. During reconstruction he worked first in his "Lincoln Study" (the Lincoln Bedroom), then in the State-War-Navy Building (the Old Executive Office Building) next door. The Truman renovation included fireproofing, supplemented by a fire-detection system in 1965.

Jutting awnings broke the lines of the South Portico—if not the full heat of summer—before President Truman added a much-discussed balcony at the second-floor level in 1948. New wooden shades, which rolled up when not in use, did not reappear after the major renovation that soon proved necessary. Trembling chandeliers, cracking plaster, and floors which sagged and swayed prompted a months-long inspection; architects and engineers found the building dangerously weakened. The outer walls stood intact, braced by steel, while the Trumans lived at Blair House and workmen carefully dismantled the interior. After bulldozers had dug a new two-story basement, rebuilding began on new foundations with new load-bearing materials. By October 9, 1951, a crew was laying subflooring in the second-story corridor. After 27 months' work, with historic items painstakingly replaced, the Trumans moved back into the White House on March 27, 1952.

NATIONAL ARCHIVES

148

President Truman hoped to furnish the White House with items from its past and with fine antiques. His relations with Congress were often stormy; the budget proved inadequate. He did, however, receive some antiques as gifts. With television, President Truman—and later Mrs. John F. Kennedy—guided fellow citizens through the White House room by room, and public interest in its interior increased perceptibly.

During Dwight D. Eisenhower's second term, the Biddle vermeil collection was bequeathed to the White House, and in 1960 the Diplomatic Reception Room was refurnished in the style of the Federal period.

Early in 1961, Mrs. Kennedy undertook to acquire appropriate items, forming the Fine Arts Committee for the White House. Museum experts and a curatorial staff assisted its work. A Special Committee on Paintings soon followed.

In the third-floor solarium, an enlarged version of Mrs. Coolidge's "sky parlor," a decorating team hangs new chintz draperies and sorts out a new set of casual bamboo furniture on February 14, 1952.

In September 1961, the 87th Congress passed legislation providing that furniture of "historic or artistic interest" might become "inalienable" property of the mansion, with provision for the Smithsonian Institution to hold on loan any object not on display or in use. In the Ground Floor Corridor and the "principal public rooms" of the first floor, it recognized a "museum character" worthy of "primary attention."

By Executive Order, on March 7, 1964, President Lyndon B. Johnson established the Committee for the Preservation of the White House. Its duties include making "recommendations as to the articles of furniture . . . which shall be used or displayed in the public rooms . . . and as to the decor and arrangements best suited to enhance the historic and artistic values of the White House." This order also provided for a permanent curator.

During the Nixon Administration, the White House acquired for its collection numerous valuable pieces of furniture and several portraits from life of Presidents and First Ladies. Over a five-year period beginning in 1969, all of the principal rooms on the State Floor and Ground Floor were redecorated. President and Mrs. Gerald R. Ford in turn supported efforts toward the preservation of the historic character of the Presidential Mansion.

Work began on stripping the Residence's exterior walls of some 42

Red damask—pierced for sconces—shimmers on parlor walls, caryatids of Carrara marble stand unscarred, and on March 20, 1952, skilled hands lift a portrait of Wilson as the Red Room assumes its elegance again.

coats of paint and restoring the carved stonework during the Carter Administration, a project scheduled for completion in 1995. The White House also received 34 American paintings for its permanent collection.

Interest in the White House stimulated by Mrs. Ronald Reagan made possible a major redecoration of second- and third-floor rooms, as well as preservation projects on the State Floor. In 1989, President and Mrs. Bush's televised tour of the second-floor family quarters introduced a large audience to parts of the Residence rarely seen by the public.

President and Mrs. Clinton take great interest in White House history and enjoy sharing the Executive Mansion with friends, family, and the American public. Mrs. Clinton is an active participant on the Committee for the Preservation of the White House.

Donors all over the country who have given articles of museum quality to the White House can assume with confidence that the care of their gifts has become a public trust. Today the Office of the Curator not only oversees the preservation of White House treasures but also maintains a computer inventory that includes their origin, acquisition, associations with historical figures, location, and condition.

Future generations can expect data more exact than the associations that clustered around Jackson's Mexican chair or the memoirs that happened to mention such furnishings. A list compiled in April 1898, with the help of usher Thomas F. Pendel, illustrates the uncertainties of tradition and the pathos of memory: for the State Dining Room, "Brass pheasant with chicks—Mrs. Grant. . . . Set of chairs—straight pieces in back—New York City—Arthur. Side board & side table before Lincoln. Plateau—T. J.(?). White marble mantels—there since house was built." The plateau in fact dated from 1817, the mantels from 1818.

Since 1798, the White House has been painted regularly to maintain a bright white facade. By 1976, thick layers of paint had caked over some of the architectural details and prevented fresh coats from adhering to the surface. Experts were called upon to develop a system to remove the old paint safely. As the layers of paint were removed, details of the late 18th-century stonework came to light.

For generations, Americans considering the White House judged it with reference to two distinct norms: a great palace of Europe (whether seen or imagined) and the home of a gentleman (a standard that altered rapidly indeed). These criteria diverged so widely that defining an ideal Executive Mansion was not easy—though of course every citizen and visitor freely passed judgment.

In 1834 a thoughtful, anonymous writer spoke gravely to the point: "This is the only PALACE in the United States. The chief magistrate of the United States has justly a spacious house, while in office, at the charge of the nation, and for the honor of the nation; and yet we cannot but hope, that as little of European parade and display, and especially of luxury or extravagance, will be found there in future, as in years past since our republic was founded."

Now the White House ranks as a norm in its own right. Comparisons still come naturally, though less obviously: The number of rooms in the family suite—12—approximates the number in a large suburban home. But the ritual of state occasions speaks not for individual but for national dignity. Suited to its time, as George Washington hoped, in established maturity the White House looks "beyond the present day."

THE PRESIDENT'S PARK: *This drawing is based on an aerial photograph and on a plan drawn by the National Park Service. Numbered trees and gardens are associated with Presidents or First Ladies. The key at right identifies trees planted by President and Mrs. Clinton and others by the name of the President in office when they were planted.*

Jefferson Mounds

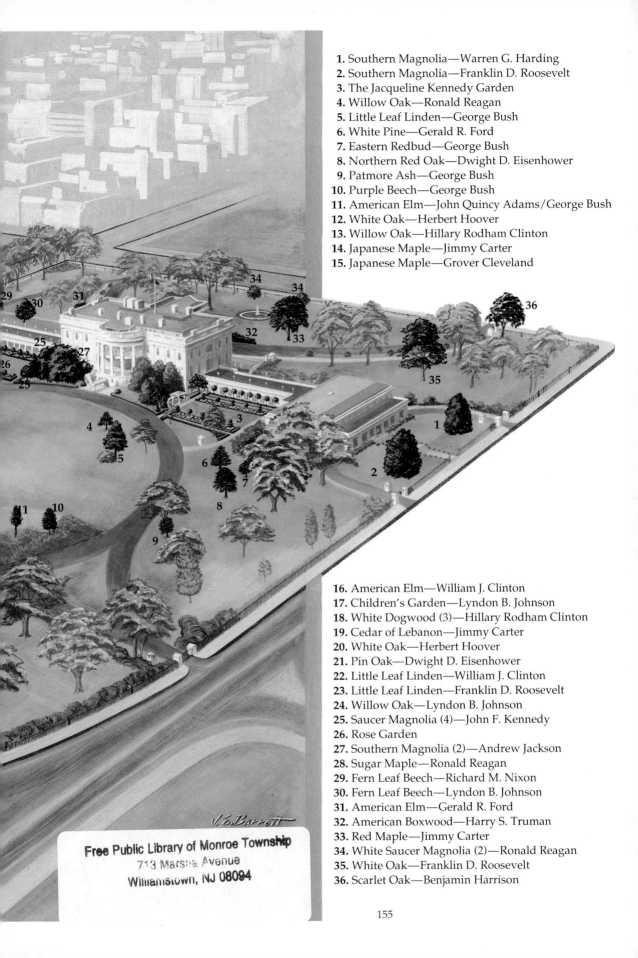

1. Southern Magnolia—Warren G. Harding
2. Southern Magnolia—Franklin D. Roosevelt
3. The Jacqueline Kennedy Garden
4. Willow Oak—Ronald Reagan
5. Little Leaf Linden—George Bush
6. White Pine—Gerald R. Ford
7. Eastern Redbud—George Bush
8. Northern Red Oak—Dwight D. Eisenhower
9. Patmore Ash—George Bush
10. Purple Beech—George Bush
11. American Elm—John Quincy Adams/George Bush
12. White Oak—Herbert Hoover
13. Willow Oak—Hillary Rodham Clinton
14. Japanese Maple—Jimmy Carter
15. Japanese Maple—Grover Cleveland

16. American Elm—William J. Clinton
17. Children's Garden—Lyndon B. Johnson
18. White Dogwood (3)—Hillary Rodham Clinton
19. Cedar of Lebanon—Jimmy Carter
20. White Oak—Herbert Hoover
21. Pin Oak—Dwight D. Eisenhower
22. Little Leaf Linden—William J. Clinton
23. Little Leaf Linden—Franklin D. Roosevelt
24. Willow Oak—Lyndon B. Johnson
25. Saucer Magnolia (4)—John F. Kennedy
26. Rose Garden
27. Southern Magnolia (2)—Andrew Jackson
28. Sugar Maple—Ronald Reagan
29. Fern Leaf Beech—Richard M. Nixon
30. Fern Leaf Beech—Lyndon B. Johnson
31. American Elm—Gerald R. Ford
32. American Boxwood—Harry S. Truman
33. Red Maple—Jimmy Carter
34. White Saucer Magnolia (2)—Ronald Reagan
35. White Oak—Franklin D. Roosevelt
36. Scarlet Oak—Benjamin Harrison

INDEX

Boldface indicates illustrations

Additional References

The reader may wish to consult books on or by individual Presidents and their families for information on the White House during specific administrations, as well as the following books, periodical, and research sources for material related to the White House:

Books: Lonnelle Aikman, *The Living White House*, 1991; Frank Freidel, *The Presidents of the United States*, 1994; Frank Freidel and William Pencak, editors, *The White House: The First Two Hundred Years*, 1994; Bess Furman, *White House Profile*, 1951; Amy La Follette Jensen, *The White House and its thirty-five families*, 1971; Elise K. Kirk, *Music at the White House: A History of the American Spirit*, 1986; Margaret Brown Klapthor, *The First Ladies*, 1994, and *Official White House China: 1789 to the Present*, 1975; William Kloss and others, *Art in the White House: A Nation's Pride*, 1992; Kenneth W. Leish, *The White House*, 1972; William Ryan and Desmond Guinness, *The White House: An Architectural History*, 1980; William Seale, *The President's House: A History* (2 volumes), 1986, and *The White House: The History of an American Idea*, 1992; Esther Singleton, *The Story of the White House* (2 volumes), 1907; Marie Smith, *Entertaining at the White House*, 1967; Jane Shadel Spillman, *White House Glassware: Two Centuries of Presidential Entertaining*, 1989; U. S. Commission on the Renovation of the Executive Mansion, *Report . . .*, 1952; J. B. West, *Upstairs at the White House*, 1973.
Periodical: *White House History*, Volume One, 1983.
Research Sources: Mary-Jane M. Dowd, compiler, *Records of the Office of Public Buildings and Public Parks of the National Capital—Record Group 42, Inventory No. 16*, National Archives and Records Administration, 1992; John Guidas and others, *The White House: Resources for Research at the Library of Congress*, The Library of Congress, 1992.

Composition for *The White House: An Historic Guide* by the Typographic section of National Geographic Production Services, Pre-Press Division. Printed and bound by R. R. Donnelly & Sons Co., Willard, Ohio. Color separations by Lanman Progressive Co., Washington, D.C. Cover and dust jacket printed by Southeastern Color Graphics, Inc., Johnson City, Tenn.